First published in 2022 by Miles Kelly Publishing Ltd
Harding's Barn, Bardfield End Green, Thaxted, Essex, CM6 3PX, UK
Copyright © Miles Kelly Publishing Ltd 2022

2 4 6 8 10 9 7 5 3 1

Publishing Director Belinda Gallagher
Creative Director Jo Cowan
Editorial Director Rosie Neave
Senior Editors Fran Bromage, Sarah Carpenter, Amy Johnson
Design Manager Simon Lee
Designers Joe Jones, Andrea Slane, Rob Hale
Image Manager Liberty Newton
Production Jennifer Brunwin
Reprographics Stephan Davis
Assets Lorraine King
Consultants Clint Twist, Anne Rooney, Steve Parker

All rights reserved. No part of this publication may be reproduced, stored in a retrieval system, or transmitted by any means, electronic, mechanical, photocopying, recording or otherwise, without the prior permission of the copyright holder.

ISBN 978-1-78989-559-9

Printed in China

British Library Cataloguing-in-Publication Data
A catalogue record for this book is available from the British Library

Made with paper from a sustainable forest

www.mileskelly.net

IMPORTANT NOTICE
The publisher and author cannot be held responsible for any injuries, damage or loss resulting from the use or misuse of any of the information in this book.

How to use the projects

This book is packed full of amazing facts about science. There are also 46 cool projects, designed to make the subject come alive.

Before you start a project:
- Always ask an adult to help you.
- Read the instructions carefully.
- Gather all the supplies you need.
- Clear a surface to work on and cover it with newspaper.

- Wear an apron or old t-shirt to protect your clothing.

Notes for helpers:
- Children will need supervision for the projects, usually because they require the use of scissors, or preparation beforehand.
- Read the instructions together before starting and help to gather the equipment.

SAFETY FIRST!
Be careful when using glue or anything sharp, such as scissors.

How to use/How it works
If your project doesn't work the first time, try again – just have fun!

Supplies
The equipment should be easy to find, around the house or from a craft store. Always ask before using materials from home.

Numbered stages
Each stage of the project is numbered and illustrated. Follow the stages in the order shown to complete the project. If glue or paint is used, make sure it is dry before moving onto the next stage.

The big freeze

The temperature at which a substance freezes can vary. In this project you can see how salt affects the freezing point of water.

HOW IT WORKS
The tub with salt does not freeze because the salt lowers the water's freezing point.

SUPPLIES
two plastic food tubs • salt • spoon
warm water • marker pen • freezer

WHAT TO DO
1. Fill each tub halfway with warm water.

2. Stir salt into one of the tubs. Keep adding salt until no more will dissolve. Mark the tub that has salt.

3. Put both tubs into the freezer. Check them every two or three hours. What do you notice?

Science 12-41

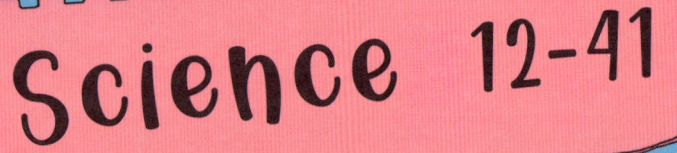

- **14** Energize!
  - 15 Energy swing
- **16** Force and motion
  - 17 Reaction rocket
- **18** Pulling together
  - 18 Parachute power
- **20** Pushing it
  - 21 Bottle crusher
- **22** Floating and flying
  - 23 Sink or float!
- **24** The littlest things
- **26** It's chemistry
- **28** Ordering the elements
- **30** What's the matter?
  - 31 The big freeze
- **32** Getting a reaction
  - 33 Make an explosion!
- **34** Sparks flying
  - 35 Static shake
- **36** Magnetize!
  - 37 Make a compass
- **38** Lighten up
  - 39 Build a periscope
- **40** Sounding out
  - 41 Water music

Space 42-71

44	What is space?	58	Further away
45	Paper moon		
46	Big Bang!	60	Super star
47	Puffed-up universe	61	Eclipse kit
48	Super sizzlers	62	Rocky worlds
49	Twinkle, twinkle, little star	63	Exploding volcano
50	Star cities	64	Gassy giants
51	Galactic art	65	Speedy planets
52	Gas and dust	66	Space rocks
53	Looking for nebulae	67	Space rock hunt
54	Greedy galaxy	68	Cosmic snowballs
		69	A tale of tails
56	The Sun's family	70	Exploring space
		71	Balloon rocket

Earth 72-105

74 The living planet
 75 Big bang
76 Dynamic Earth
 77 Chocolate planet
78 Explosive eruptions
 79 Make a mud-flow
80 Rattle and roll
 81 Make a seismometer
82 Water world
 83 Disappearing act
84 Early life
86 What is a biome?
88 Precious places
90 The water cycle
 90 Make a mini water cycle

92 Air and atmosphere
 93 Lightning strikes
94 Extreme weather
 94 Tornado in a bottle
96 Weather science
 97 Build a barometer
98 Earth's resources
 99 Rock cakes
100 Powering the planet
 101 Potato power!
102 Reduce, reuse, recycle
 102 Help the Earth picture
104 Can climate change?
 105 Be a weather historian

Body 106-135

- **108** Outside in
  - 109 Sun stoppers
- **110** Air bags
  - 111 Model lungs
- **112** Pump it!
  - 113 Listen to the beat
- **114** Down the hatch
  - 114 Enzyme breakdown
- **116** Water works
  - 117 Saving blood
- **118** Pulling together
- **120** Super skeleton
- **122** Bone idol
- **124** Brilliant brain
  - 124 Where's that letter?
- **126** Get the message
  - 127 Test your reflexes
- **128** All eyes
  - 129 Make a stereoscope
- **130** Sound system
  - 130 Super sound waves
- **132** Super senses
  - 133 Test your taste
- **134** To the rescue!
  - 135 Make fake mucus

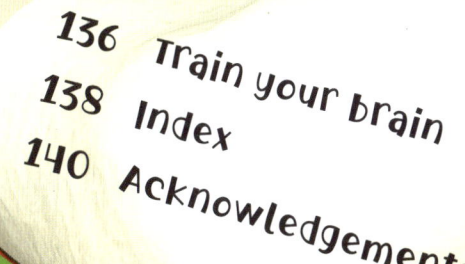

- **136** Train your brain
- **138** Index
- **140** Acknowledgements

Energize!

Energy is what you need to make things happen. Scientists say it is the ability to perform 'work'. It takes many forms, but you can't either create it or destroy it. When you use energy, you simply swap it to another form.

READY OR HAPPENING?

There are two kinds of energy. Kinetic energy (KE) is energy actually doing something. It is the energy things have when they're moving. Potential energy (PE) is energy that could do something. If you're high up, for instance, you have PE, because gravity can pull you down.

▼ The Shockwave jet-powered truck can scorch along at over 600 km/h. Moving this monster so fast involves a LOT of energy.

1 Chemical energy is stored in the chemical bonds of the jet fuel (PE).

2 As the engines burn the fuel, the chemical energy bursts out as heat energy. Heat makes gases swell and generates the thrust that drives the truck forwards.

HEAT AND TEMPERATURE

Heat is the energy of molecules (tiny particles) moving. The faster they move, the hotter things are. Temperature is the way you measure how hot things are. The faster molecules move, the hotter it gets and the higher the temperature.

Extreme degrees

The lowest possible temperature is **−273.15°C**, which is called **absolute zero**.

The highest temperature known in nature is about **10 billion°C**, in large exploding stars (supernovae).

The lowest temperature recorded on Earth was **−89°C**, in Antarctica. The highest was **56.7°C**, in Death Valley, USA.

Energy swing

You can explore the relationship between kinetic energy (KE) and potential energy (PE) with a swing. The idea is to spot when the conversions between KE and PE occur.

WHAT TO DO

1. Sit still on a swing. You currently have stored energy (PE) in your muscles.

2. Now push off with your leg muscles and move your body to help you swing higher. You are converting the PE of your muscles into the KE of movement.

3. By moving your body, you can gain enough momentum to swing high. As you swing up, the KE turns into PE – the energy gravity gives because of your height.

4. At the highest point of your swing, you run out of KE and can go no higher. But you have built up a lot of PE.

5. As you swing back down again and pick up speed, the PE is converted to KE. The KE will carry you right back up the other side and you will build up PE again.

3 As the truck accelerates, the heat energy changes to KE.

WHERE DO WE GET ENERGY?

Most of the energy we use to live our lives comes from burning coal, oil and gas. These 'fossil fuels' are made from remains of living things. Burning them causes pollution, and supplies will eventually run out. So more people are using cleaner renewable energy.

▶ Renewable energy sources can be used again and again and will not run out.

Wind

Giant blades turned by the wind drive electricity generators

Solar

Photovoltaic (PV) cells convert sunlight into electricity

Force and motion

A force is a push or pull. It changes the speed, direction or shape of something. Objects have natural inertia – they only move when forced. Once moving, they have momentum, meaning they move at the same speed and direction until forced to change.

MOTION RULES!

In the 1600s, the great scientist Sir Isaac Newton came up with three rules about force and movement, known as the Laws of Motion:

1. Things only accelerate or decelerate when forced to.
2. The acceleration depends on how strong the force is and how great the mass being accelerated is.
3. Every force or action is balanced by an equal force in the opposite direction.

FIRST LAW
Booster rockets provide the force needed to launch a space rocket from the ground. Once it reaches the right speed the boosters can be jettisoned.

SECOND LAW
Space scientists can use Newton's law to work out just how much rocket power they will need to lift (accelerate) a certain weight, or payload.

▶ To get a spacecraft into space, it has to get moving fast enough to overcome Earth's gravity.

GETTING THE GS

Extreme accelerations are sometimes measured in 'g's – that is, how they compare to the acceleration when you fall due to gravity. A top-fuel dragster can accelerate from zero to 160 km/h in 0.86 seconds. That is a horizontal acceleration of 5.3 g – 5.3 times faster than you fall!

THIRD LAW
A rocket can move through empty space even though it seems to have nothing to push against. As burning gases swell out from the engines, they push against the rocket. So the rocket is pushed forward just as much as the gases are pushed back.

▼ Action: swelling gases produce the thrust that pushes the rocket forward.

▼ Reaction: rocket produces an equal thrust force, pushing the gases backward.

Reaction rocket

A rocket is propelled by the action and reaction between the rocket body and the fuel. In the same way, this water rocket is propelled by the reaction force between the water and the air you pump in to the bottle. Make sure an adult helps you with this project.

SUPPLIES
plastic soft drinks bottle • cork that fits snugly into the mouth of the bottle • long thin screw and screwdriver • bicycle pump plus needle adaptor for inflating balls • strong glue or adhesive tape • thick card • scissors

HOW TO MAKE
1. Using the screw, carefully make a hole in the cork that fits the needle adaptor snugly, and push the adaptor in – it needs to go all the way through.

2. Cut out three fins from the card. Stick them securely to the top of the bottle using the glue or tape.

3. Quarter-fill the bottle with water, insert the cork and connect the pump.

4. Take your rocket to an open space and stand it upside down on the fins.

5. Keeping your face clear, pump air in. Pressure will build up until your rocket blasts off!

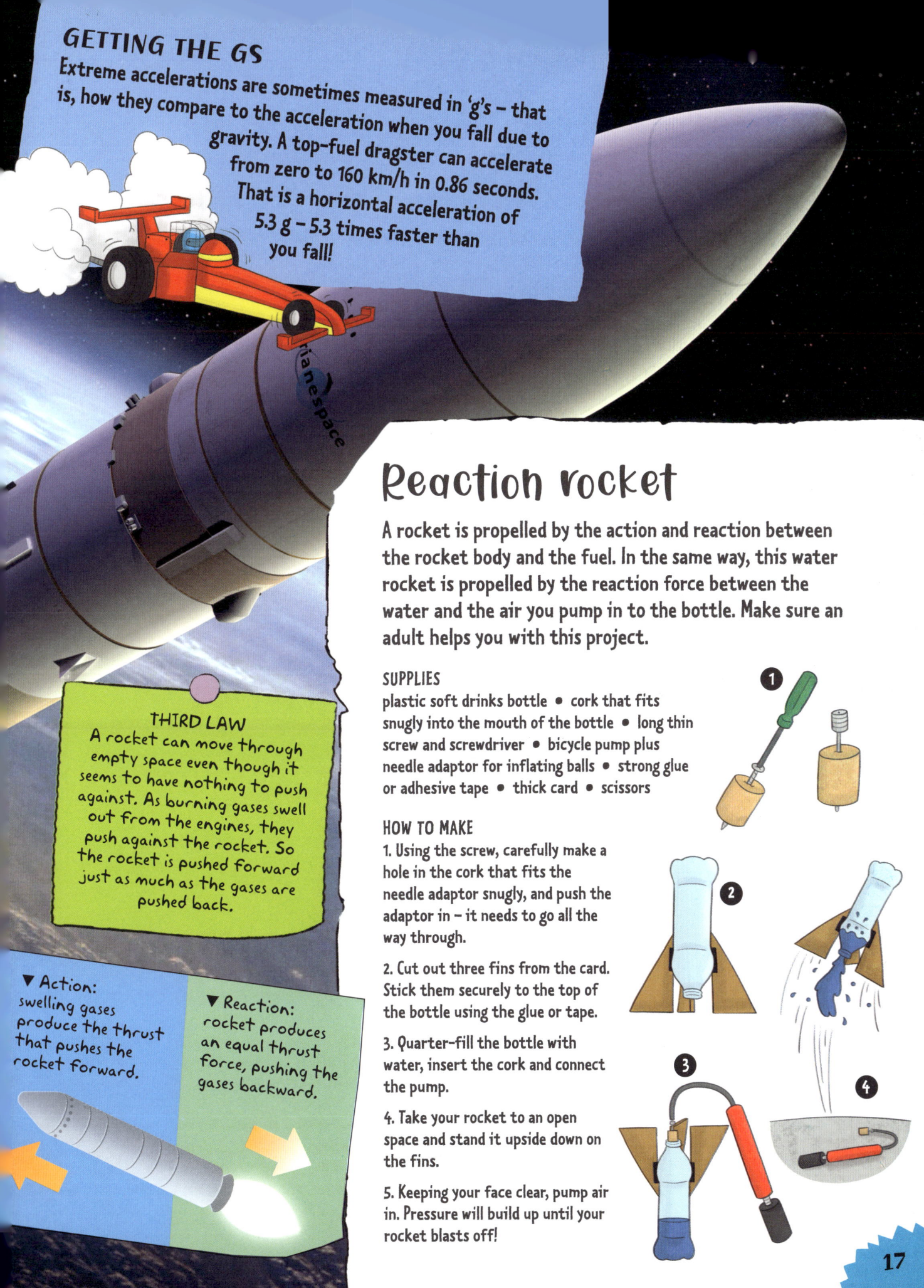

Pulling together

When you drop something, it doesn't just fall of its own accord. It falls because it is pulled towards Earth by a force called gravity. Gravity is what keeps us on the ground, and why the planets go round the Sun.

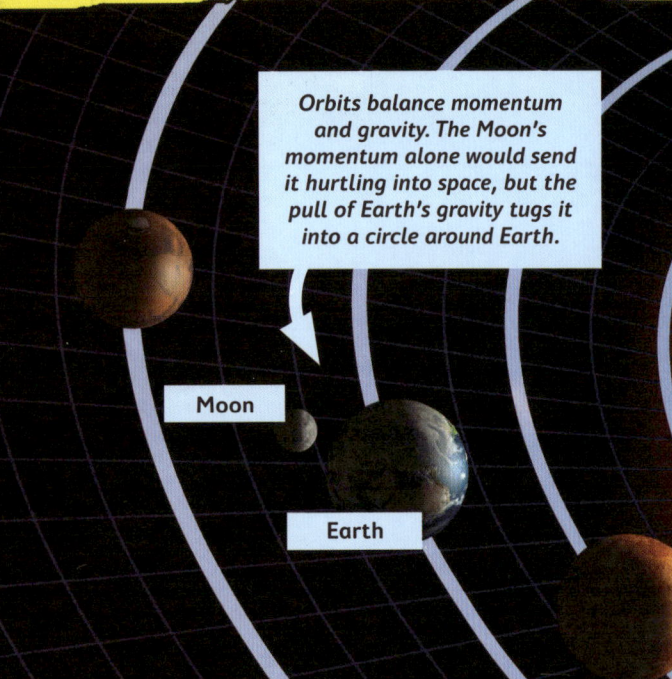

Orbits balance momentum and gravity. The Moon's momentum alone would send it hurtling into space, but the pull of Earth's gravity tugs it into a circle around Earth.

Moon

Earth

UNIVERSAL ATTRACTION

Gravity is the mutual force of attraction that holds the Universe together. Every bit of matter in the Universe has its own gravity pull and attracts everything else. The strength of the pull depends on how massive things are and how far apart. Objects with more mass pull more strongly than those with less.

◀ In space, things go round each other in paths called orbits. The planets in our Solar System, as well as other objects such as asteroids and comets, all orbit the Sun because it has a massive pull of gravity.

Parachute power

If there was no air, a feather would fall at the same speed as a lead weight. But air slows things down, as you can see with this simple parachute.

SUPPLIES
plastic carrier bag • ruler • pencil
scissors • thin string • two small plastic toys, roughly the same size
adhesive tape

HOW TO MAKE
1. Cut a 10 cm square from the bag. Using the scissors, make a tiny hole in each corner.
2. Thread a piece of string through each hole and tie it in place.
3. Tie or stick all four strings to one of the toys.

HOW TO USE
Find a place indoors from where you can drop the toys. Drop the toy with the parachute and the other toy at the same time. Which one reaches the ground first?

HOW IT WORKS
The toy with the parachute takes longer to reach the ground because the parachute's large area means it hits a lot of air as it falls, slowing it down.

HEAVY!

When something is heavy, you might talk of its weight. But scientists talk only of mass. Mass is how much matter there is. For scientists, weight is a force; it's how strongly gravity pulls. Weight is measured as a force in units called newtons, whereas pounds and kilograms are measures of mass. So weightlifters should be called masslifters!

TOP OF THE WORLD

In 2012, daredevil skydiver Felix Baumgartner jumped from a capsule 39 km above the ground. When he first started to fall, he accelerated rapidly, reaching 1357.64 km/h. The force of the air pushing on him (air resistance) increased as he gained speed. Eventually the air resistance became equal to his weight, and he then fell steadily at the same speed, called terminal velocity.

DROPPED!

You might expect heavier objects to fall faster, but Earth's gravity accelerates everything down equally fast.

▶ It's said that the scientist Galileo Galilei (1564–1642) proved this by dropping two different weights off the leaning Tower of Pisa – and found they reached the ground simultaneously.

◀ Jumping from the top of the stratosphere, it took just over 9 minutes for Baumgartner to reach the ground.

Pushing it

Pressure is the amount of force acting over an area. Air and water exert pressure as they are always pushing against their surroundings. This is the combined effect of the molecules in water and air constantly moving, whizzing around at speeds of 1500 km/h or more.

Pressure Planet

The planet Venus has such a thick atmosphere that its pressure is **90 times** that of Earth's.

Robot vehicles may be sent to land on Venus in the future.

Venus rovers will need to be built **super strong** to avoid being quickly crushed.

UNDER PRESSURE

When you squeeze water or air molecules into a smaller space, the molecules jostle harder and the pressure rises. Similarly, adding heat increases pressure as the molecules zoom about faster and smash into things more forcefully. In a geyser, underground water is superheated and squeezed into very small spaces, creating great pressure.

▶ Geysers are found near active volcanic areas where there is magma (molten rock) underground. The magma superheats the water, creating enough pressure to shoot out a scalding jet at the surface.

Bottle crusher

We are so used to air pressure that it's hard to imagine its power. But you can witness it for yourself in this simple experiment with steam in a bottle. It's crushing!

SUPPLIES
plastic soft drinks bottle with a screw top • a little hot water • cold or iced water

WHAT TO DO
1. Ask an adult to quarter-fill the bottle with really hot water from a tap or kettle.

2. Leave to stand for a few seconds, then screw the lid on tight.

3. Hold the bottle under a running cold tap, or place in a bowl of iced water. The bottle will instantly be crushed.

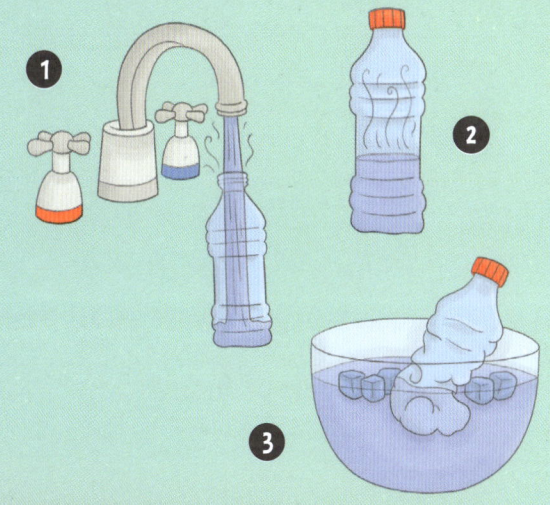

HOW IT WORKS
As the cold water chills the hot air inside the bottle, the air shrinks. The pressure of the air outside instantly crushes the bottle.

KEY

1. Groundwater seeps down through tiny channels in the rock. The water comes from rain, snow and often nearby rivers and lakes.

2. The pressure increases as the water travels further below the surface.

3. Heat from the magma chamber heats the water. Under such pressure, water reaches very high temperatures but does not boil — this is called superheating.

4. The water rises rapidly, forced through a kind of underground plumbing system of narrow channels and cracks in the rock.

5. Water and steam collect in chambers. The steam bubbles out slowly, heating the water above. The water boils suddenly, releasing pressure and spewing out water and steam.

6. In a hot spring, rising water is cooled by groundwater before reaching the surface. The pressure drops, so the water flows out steadily rather than erupting.

DRIVING WINDS

Weather forecasters monitor variations in pressure in the air closely, because pressure variations are what makes our weather and drives all winds. When the air gets cold in one place and sinks, the pressure increases. That pushes air towards low pressure areas where the air is warmer and rising.

▶ In this satellite image, clouds reveal the spiral pattern of winds circulating a low pressure zone.

21

Floating and flying

It's amazing that heavy aeroplanes can fly, and big ships can float. After all, even a tiny stone will fall through the air and sink in water. But both planes and ships use their shape to maximize the support given by molecules, which give lift in air and buoyancy in water.

ON THE SURFACE

When an object is submerged in water, it's pulled down by its weight. But the water pushes back up with a buoyancy force equal to the weight of water displaced (pushed out of the way) by the object. If the object is less dense than water, it floats. It is said to be buoyant.

1 Boat displaces a certain volume of water

2 Displaced water causes a buoyancy force

3 When the weight of the displaced water equals the weight of the boat, the boat floats

▲ A heavy metal ship can float because its large hull pushes enough water out of the way to create a huge upthrust, enough to keep it afloat. The key is the air trapped inside the hull, which reduces the ship's overall density.

◀ Burners add more hot air whenever the balloon needs to climb.

FLOATING ON AIR

Just as ships can float on water, so balloons can float on air. Here the balloon must be filled with a gas that is less dense than air. That way the balloon becomes naturally buoyant and rises through the air, just like a cork bobs up through water. The gas in the balloon could be helium, which is lighter than air, or hot air, which is lighter than cool air.

GIVING A LIFT

The wings of a plane have a special downcurve to slice through the air at an angle, a shape known as an aerofoil. This diverts the flow of air over and under the wings in a special way and alters how the air pushes on the wing. It pushes less on top of the wing and more from beneath, and so the wing is lifted.

▶ If you look at a plane wing side-on, you can see the aerofoil shape. It has a curved topside and a flat or curved underside.

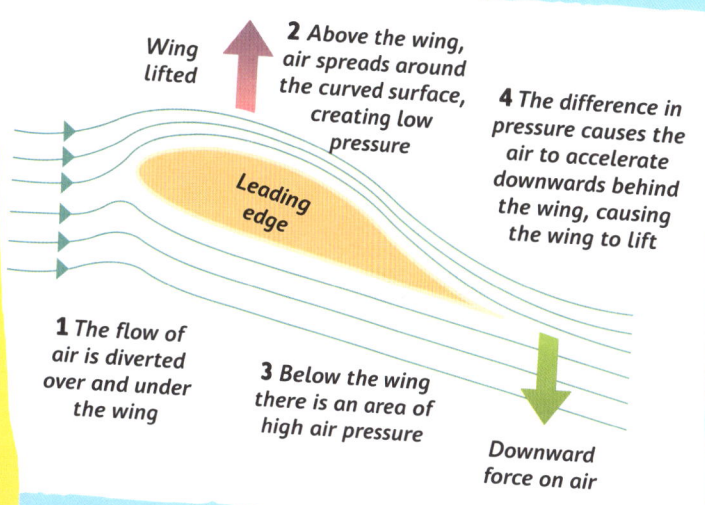

FORCES OF FLIGHT

Planes fly by precisely balancing thrust, drag, gravity and lift. Lift is created by the continuous movement of the wings through the air. The faster they move, and the steeper the angle at which they attack the air, the greater the lift. A pilot can get extra lift by increasing the power of the engines to boost thrust, or by using the wing flaps to steepen the angle.

◀ To keep a plane flying steadily, thrust must equal drag, and lift must equal weight.

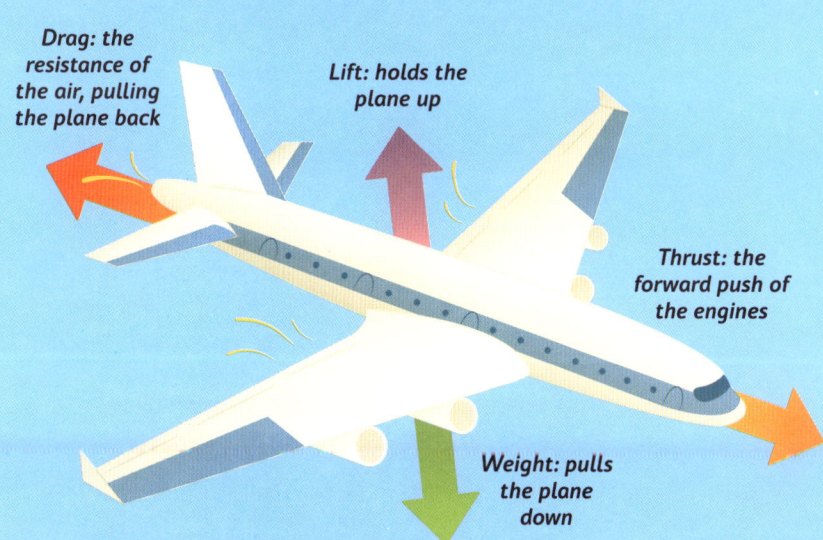

Sink or float!

See how shape can give a boat buoyancy by reshaping a ball of modelling clay into a boat that floats.

SUPPLIES
modelling clay • basin or large bowl of cold water

WHAT TO DO
1. Lower a large ball of modelling clay into the water.

2. You will see that the ball sinks – this is because it is denser than water. The water level rises because water is displaced by the ball as it sinks.

3. Take the ball out and reshape it to make a bowl-shaped boat with tall sides.

4. Place the clay back in the water. This time it should float, even though it has the same weight. This is because the shape displaces a larger volume of water, due to the air it contains.

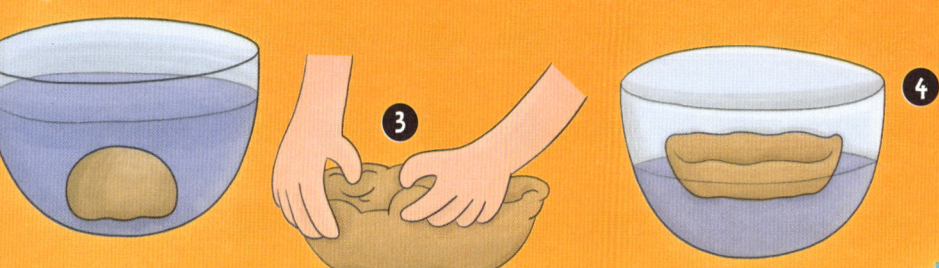

The littlest things

All matter is built up from tiny pieces called atoms. Atoms are so tiny that two billion could fit on this full stop. Scientists once thought atoms were the smallest things of all, but it was then discovered that they are actually more like clouds — mostly empty space, dotted with even tinier 'subatomic particles'.

INSIDE AN ATOM

At the core of every atom is its nucleus, a cluster of two kinds of particle: protons and neutrons. Even tinier particles, electrons, whizz around the nucleus. But don't imagine subatomic particles as tiny solid balls; they are just concentrations of energy that occur in particular places.

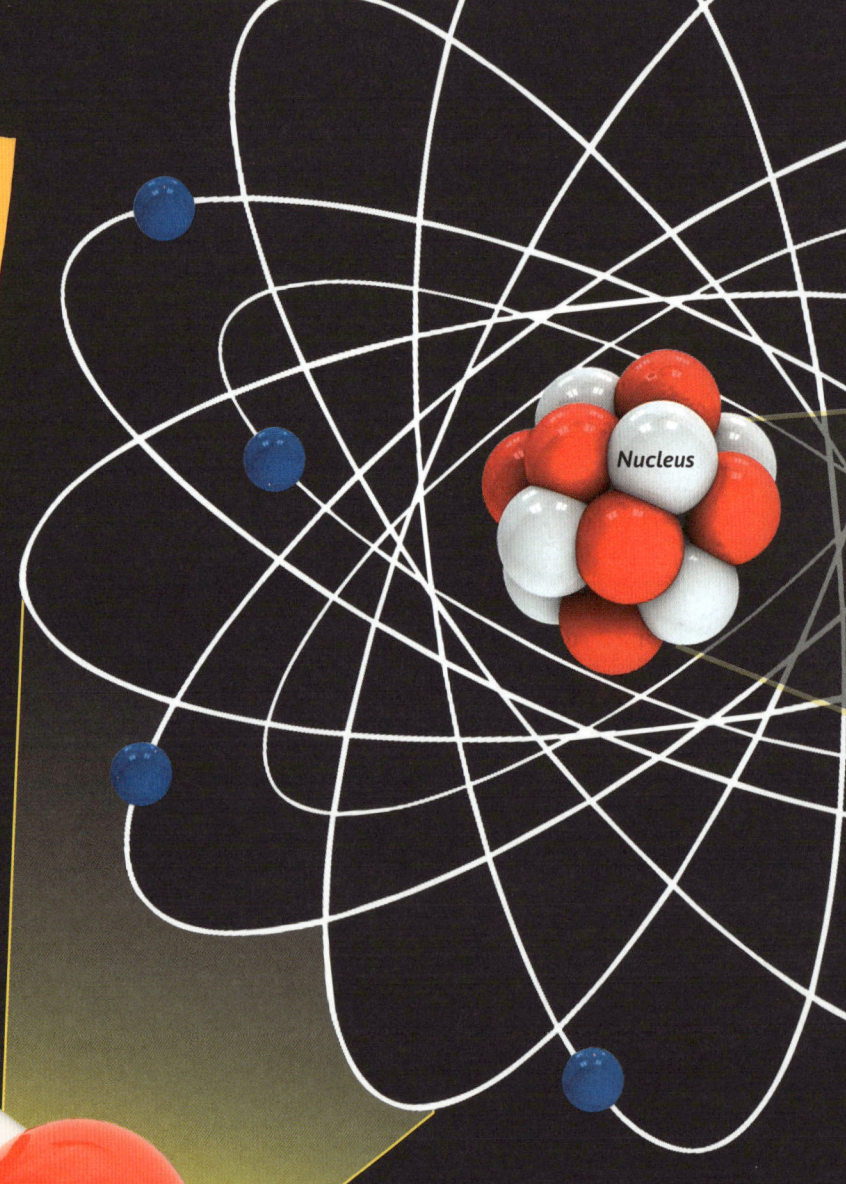

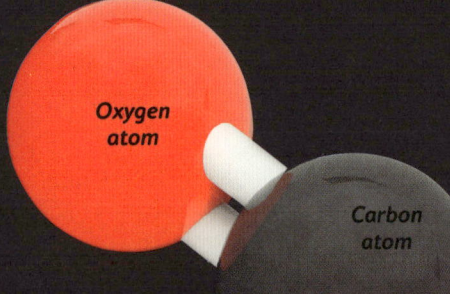

▶ A molecule is made up of two or more atoms chemically bonded together. In this carbon dioxide molecule, a carbon atom is bonded to two oxygen atoms.

▲ The number of electrons in an atom always matches the number of protons, so an atom has a neutral electrical charge. There are eight protons and eight electrons in this oxygen atom.

FOUR FORCES

Atoms can be split, but they are usually held together by three forces – the electrical attraction between the negative electrons and positive protons and the 'strong' and 'weak' forces that bind the particles of the nucleus together. These three forces, together with gravity, are the basic forces of nature that hold the entire Universe together.

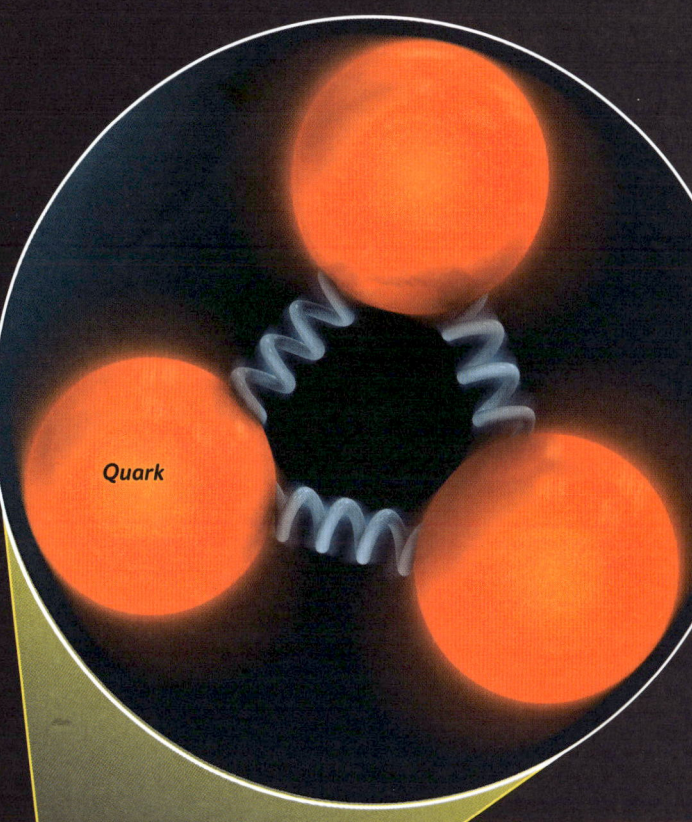

Quark

Electrons have a negative electrical charge

▶ The nucleus of an oxygen atom.

▲ A proton composed of three quarks. Quarks are a very important type of particle, as they combine to make up protons and neutrons.

Proton

Neutron

Scientists now have **microscopes** powerful enough to actually see **atoms**.

Protons have a positive electrical charge; neutrons have none

The tiniest of all

By smashing atoms together at high speeds, scientists have discovered 200 different subatomic particles. They're all made from two kinds: quarks and leptons. Electrons are leptons. Protons and neutrons are built up from quarks. There are six 'flavours' of quarks, and scientists have given them strange names.

 Up quark

Down quark

Top quark

 Bottom quark

Charm quark

 Strange quark

25

It's chemistry

There's an unimaginable number of different substances in the universe. Yet they are all made up from just over 100 basic chemicals, known as elements, such as gold, iron and carbon. Each element has its own unique kind of atom.

Hydrogen

The Sun consists of about 90 percent hydrogen

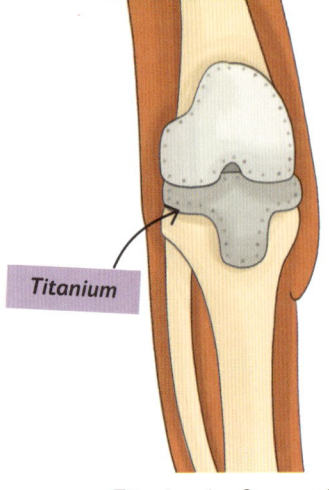

Titanium

Titanium is often used in artificial joints

Calcium

Chalk cliffs are made of the compound calcium carbonate

UNIQUE ATOMS

All the atoms of an element are the same. Each can be identified by its own atomic number. This is the number of protons in its atoms, from hydrogen, which has one to oganesson, which has 118. The number of protons is the only difference between elements, yet it has a huge effect on their nature.

MAKING WATER

An element is one type of atom. A compound is made when atoms of different elements join together. A molecule of each compound always has the same combination of atoms. For instance a water molecule is always made from two atoms of hydrogen and one of oxygen.

▼ Sea water is a mixture made up of mostly water, with a small amount of salts and other substances.

26

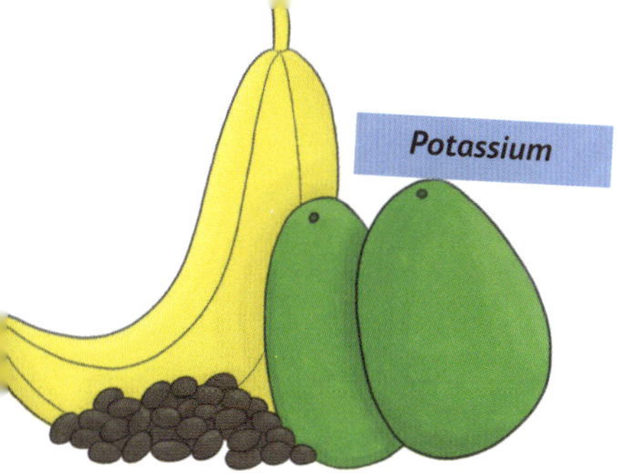

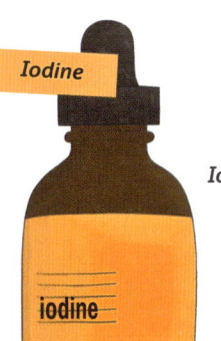
Potassium

Fruits such as avocados, raisins and bananas are high in potassium

Polonium
Radium

ELEMENTS TOGETHER
Pure elements are quite rare. Most substances are compounds — made from two or more elements bonded together. The compounds are usually very different from the elements. Salt is a compound of sodium and chlorine. But sodium is a metal that fizzes and glows in water, and chlorine is a thick green gas.

The radioactive elements polonium and radium were discovered by Marie and Pierre Curie, in 1898

Iodine

Iodine is used as a disinfectant in treating wounds

Earth's core is a solid ball of iron and nickel surrounded by a liquid outer core

Iron
Nickel

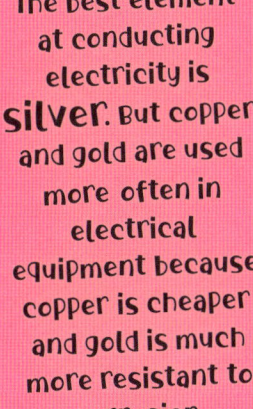

The best element at conducting electricity is **silver**. But copper and gold are used more often in electrical equipment because copper is cheaper and gold is much more resistant to corrosion.

Carbon dioxide

Plants take in carbon dioxide and use it to produce sugar for food

Aluminium is used to make many different things, including aeroplanes

Aluminium

Oxygen

Every cell in the human body needs a continual supply of oxygen

Sulphur

The gas sulphur dioxide can be released during volcanic eruptions

Noble gases such as argon and krypton are often used to fill light bulbs because they don't react with the bulb's metal filament and burn it out the way oxygen would.

Mercury

Mercury is the only metal that is liquid at room temperature

Scientists give each element a symbol, typically its initial — Carbon is C, Hydrogen is H, Copper is Cu.

27

Ordering the elements

In the 19th century, chemist Dmitri Mendeleev (1834–1907) realized that all the elements can be arranged in a chart called the Periodic Table, in order of their atomic number. Elements in the vertical columns have similar characteristics. Elements get less reactive from left to right, along the rows.

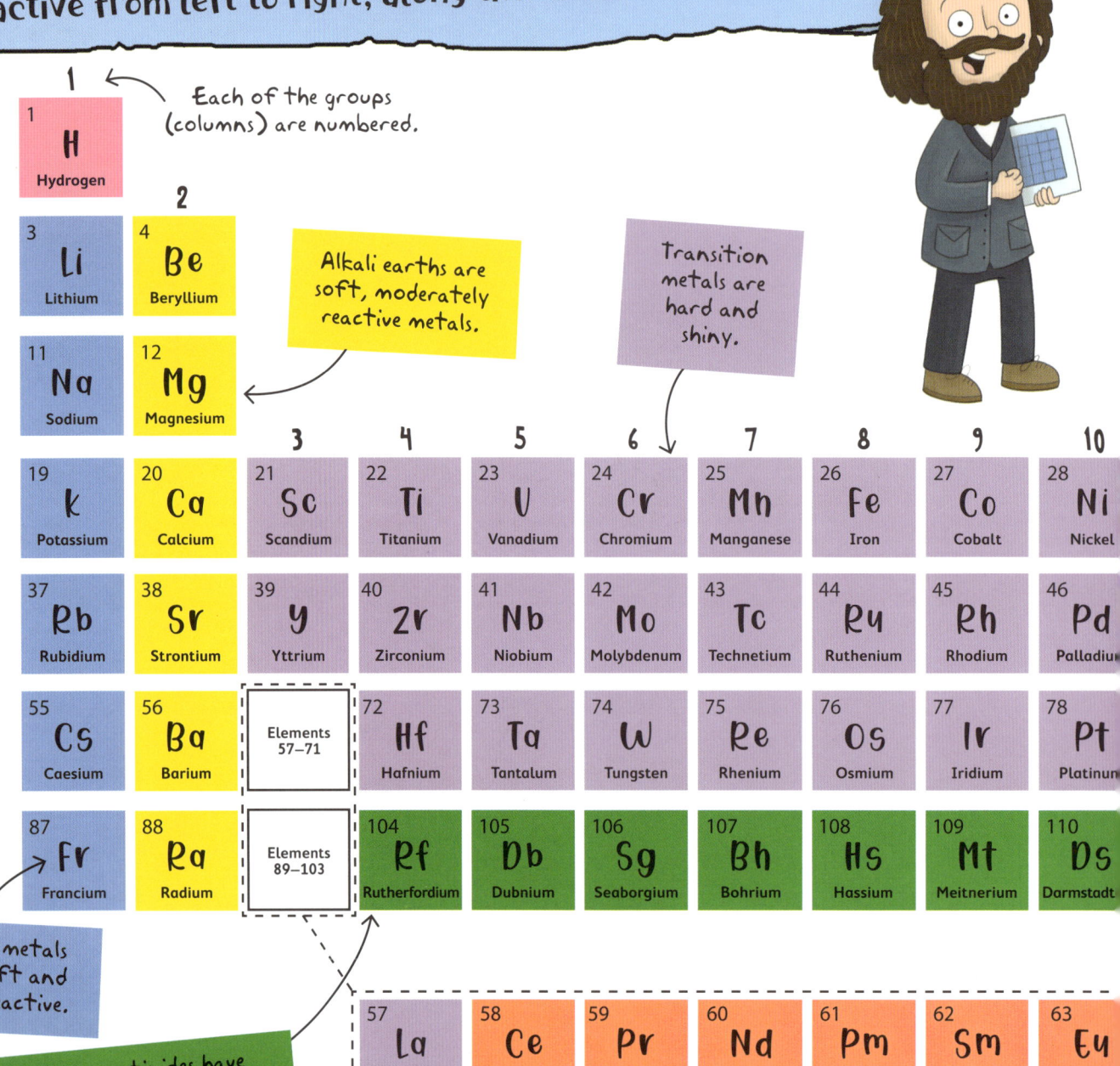

◀ Unlike the noble gases on the right, sodium, on the left of the table, is highly reactive, exploding when it hits water.

▶ A plasma ball is a glass ball filled with a mixture of noble gases. When electricity is supplied, plasma fibres, which reach from an inner electrode to the outer glass, create beams of coloured light.

Post-transition metals such as aluminium and tin are sometimes called poor metals because they are quite soft.

Other non-metals include some really important elements such as oxygen.

Halogens are all highly reactive and form acids when they join with hydrogen.

13	14	15	16	17	18
					2 He Helium
5 B Boron	6 C Carbon	7 N Nitrogen	8 O Oxygen	9 F Fluorine	10 Ne Neon
13 Al Aluminium	14 Si Silicon	15 P Phosphorus	16 S Sulphur	17 Cl Chlorine	18 Ar Argon

11	12						
29 Cu Copper	30 Zn Zinc	31 Ga Gallium	32 Ge Germanium	33 As Arsenic	34 Se Selenium	35 Br Bromine	36 Kr Krypton
47 Ag Silver	48 Cd Cadmium	49 In Indium	50 Sn Tin	51 Sb Antimony	52 Te Tellurium	53 I Iodine	54 Xe Xenon
79 Au Gold	80 Hg Mercury	81 Tl Thallium	82 Pb Lead	83 Bi Bismuth	84 Po Polonium	85 At Astatine	86 Rn Radon
111 Rg Roentgenium	112 Cn Copernicium	113 Nh Nihonium	114 Fl Flerovium	115 Mc Moscovium	116 Lv Livermorium	117 Ts Tennessine	118 Og Oganesson

Noble gases get their name because they seem to stand aloof, not reacting.

Elements 113–118 are man-made and have only been created briefly, so their properties cannot be known for certain.

Lanthanides are silvery metals, called rare earths because it was once thought they couldn't stay in the ground long without reacting.

| 64 Gd Gadolinium | 65 Tb Terbium | 66 Dy Dysprosium | 67 Ho Holmium | 68 Er Erbium | 69 Tm Thulium | 70 Yb Ytterbium | 71 Lu Lutetium |
| 96 Cm Curium | 97 Bk Berkelium | 98 Cf Californium | 99 Es Einsteinium | 100 Fm Fermium | 101 Md Mendelevium | 102 No Nobelium | 103 Lr Lawrencium |

Actinides are mostly man-made elements. They are all radioactive.

29

What's the matter?

Every substance in the universe – everything that's not just empty space – consists of matter. It has three main forms – solid, liquid and gas. These are called the states of matter. They seem different, but they can switch from one to the other and back if the temperature and pressure is right.

A gas does not have any shape or strength, and swells to fill any space. This is because the molecules move so fast that they do not hold together.

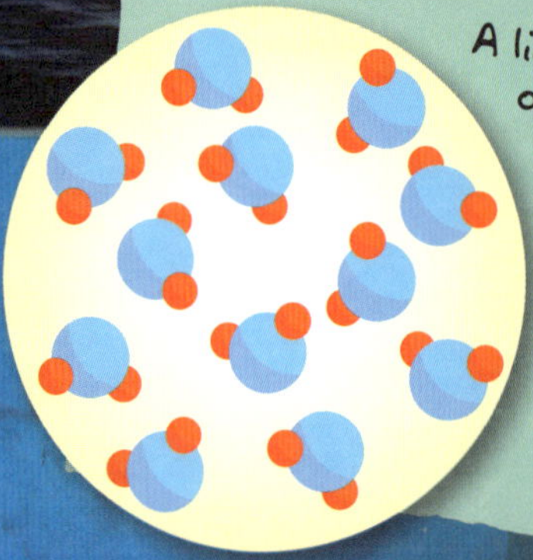

A solid has a definite shape. This is because its molecules are tightly packed and locked together in a regular structure and just vibrate on the spot. The hotter it gets, the more they vibrate.

A liquid flows and spreads out to take the shape of any container it is poured into. This is because the bonds between the molecules are loose enough to slide over each other like dry sand.

MOLECULES AND MATTER

Every substance is made of molecules. It's the way the molecules interact that makes it solid, liquid or gas. Water is one of the few substances that naturally occurs in all three states – solid as ice, liquid as water, and as a gas called water vapour. Liquid water can also be changed into a hot gas called steam by heating it until it boils.

▲ Uniquely, water expands when it freezes, so ice is less dense than water. This is why icebergs just about float.

SWITCHING STATES

As a substance warms up, its molecules move more and more. So it goes from solid to liquid (melting) and from liquid to gas (evaporation). As a substance cools down, the molecules move less and less. So they go from gas to liquid (condensing) and from liquid to solid (freezing).

▲ Gallium is a metal with a melting point of 29.8°C. This is low enough that it would melt in the palm of your hand.

Points of change

Water boils at **100°C** and freezes at **0°C**.

Helium has the lowest freezing point of any substance at **−272.2°C**.

Tungsten has the highest melting point of any metal at **3422°C**.

Carbon has the highest melting point of any substance at over **4000°C**.

PLASMA

Plasma is a fourth state of matter. It occurs when a gas gets so hot and the molecules become so energetic that they release tiny electrical charges. This makes the gas ionized (electrically charged). The Sun is mostly made up of plasma, consisting of ionized hydrogen and helium. Solar prominences are glowing loops of plasma that can erupt from its surface.

▲ Solar prominences may be 60 times as big as Earth!

The big freeze

The temperature at which a substance freezes can vary. In this project you can see how salt affects the freezing point of water.

SUPPLIES
two plastic food tubs • salt • spoon warm water • marker pen • freezer

WHAT TO DO
1. Fill each tub halfway with warm water.

2. Stir salt into one of the tubs. Keep adding salt until no more will dissolve. Mark the tub that has salt.

3. Put both tubs into the freezer. Check them every two or three hours. What do you notice?

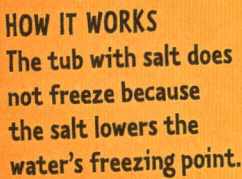

HOW IT WORKS
The tub with salt does not freeze because the salt lowers the water's freezing point.

Getting a reaction

When you see a candle burn, metal go rusty or a cake rise in the oven, you are seeing a chemical reaction. This is when different chemicals meet and react, changing each other to form new chemicals. Some reactions are slow and gentle, but some are explosive.

BURNING BRIGHT

Burning is a chemical reaction called combustion. When things burn, heat makes one substance, known as a fuel, combine chemically with oxygen. This makes a whole lot more heat. The fuel can be a solid, such as coal, a liquid like oil, or a gas such as natural gas. The oxygen usually comes from the air.

▶ Most fireworks burn a mix of charcoal, nitrate and sulphur. The charcoal is the fuel, nitrate gives oxygen and sulphur keeps it going. The paper wrapping 'pops' to produce a bang.

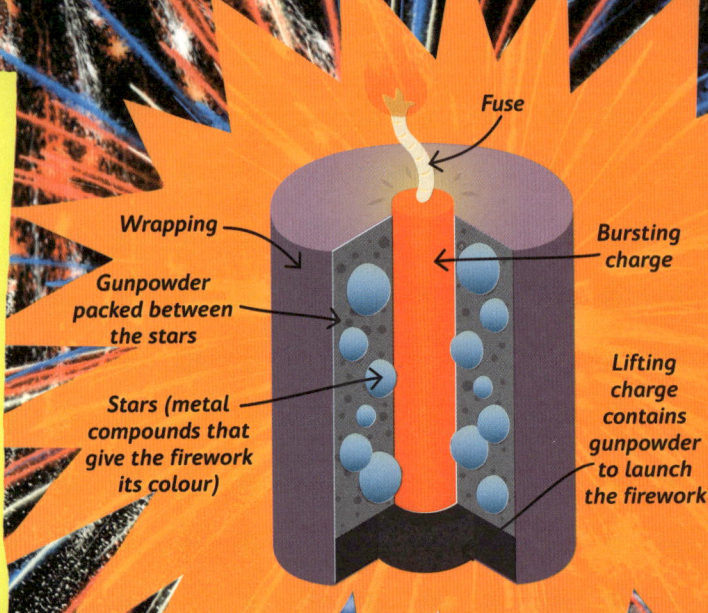

Fuse
Wrapping
Gunpowder packed between the stars
Stars (metal compounds that give the firework its colour)
Bursting charge
Lifting charge contains gunpowder to launch the firework

GOING RUSTY

Rusting, like burning, is a reaction involving oxygen. This time, though, it is a slow reaction in which iron slowly disintegrates as it reacts with water and oxygen, forming a brown crust of hydrated iron oxide. Salt water speeds this up.

▶ The nails exposed to water and oxygen (far left) and salt water and oxygen (far right) have rusted. Those in the middle have not, as they are missing water (left) or oxygen (right).

▼ Fireworks blaze in different colours because they contain traces of chemicals such as lithium (which burns red), calcium (which burns orange) and copper (which burns blue).

Make an explosion!

You can see the power of a reaction for yourself with this simple experiment. Make sure you do this with an adult watching.

SUPPLIES
tube of Mentos • one large bottle of diet fizzy drink • goggles • sheet of A4 paper large open space

WHAT TO DO
1. Go out into an open space, open the bottle and stand it on the ground.

2. Roll the paper into a simple funnel shape and place 4–6 Mentos inside.

3. Hold the funnel over the opening of the bottle and let the Mentos fall in. Now run!

HOW IT WORKS
It was once thought this explosion was a chemical reaction. But scientists now think that it is caused by microscopic pits in the surface of the Mentos. The pits encourage carbon dioxide dissolved in the fizzy drink to form gas bubbles, so it is actually a physical reaction.

▶ When nitric acid reacts with copper, it creates brown nitrogen dioxide gas and bright green copper nitrate solution.

DRAMATIC ACIDS
Strong acids are extremely dangerous because they react so powerfully. Acids contain hydrogen. When mixed with water, the hydrogen atoms are turned loose as reactive particles called ions. Acids can cause terrible skin burns. For example, sulphuric acid absorbs water in a reaction that creates heat. Strong acids also dissolve metals.

33

Sparks flying

Electricity is a form of energy. It comes from electrons – the tiny particles that whizz around the nucleus of atoms. Electrons carry a negative electrical charge, which means they have an attraction to protons, which have a positive charge. Electricity is the charge on countless electrons working together.

MOVING ELECTRICITY

Current electricity is a continuous stream of electrical charge, created by a flow of electrons that have broken free from their atoms. None move far, but the current is passed on in a kind of relay. This happens only when there is a complete circuit through which the charge can flow.

2 Wires link the parts of the circuit together, providing the pathway for the electrons to pass on the current

1 Batteries supply direct current (DC) electricity – the current only flows in one direction. If the current constantly changes direction, it is alternating current (AC). Mains electricity is an AC supply

5 When the switch is closed, the circuit is complete and the bulb can light up. This is a simple version of the circuits that power our everyday lives

HAIR RAISING

Static electricity builds up when surfaces rub together, so it can make your hair stand up when you comb it. Electrons rub off your hair onto the comb. The comb gains electrons, so it is negatively charged. Your hair has lost electrons, so is positively charged. Opposite charges attract, so your hair stands up.

LIGHTNING FLASH

Lightning occurs when ice crystals are flung together so violently by the air currents inside a thundercloud that they lose electrons, leaving them positively charged. The loose, negatively charged electrons gather at the base of the cloud — then are drawn towards any positive charge in a dramatic flash!

◀ Lightning flashes brightly because the stream of charged particles heats the air to extremely high temperatures.

◀ This simple electrical circuit has a battery to supply power, a switch to complete or break the circuit, a light bulb that glows when electricity flows, and a wire connecting them all in a loop.

3 The switch closes to complete the circuit and allow electricity to flow

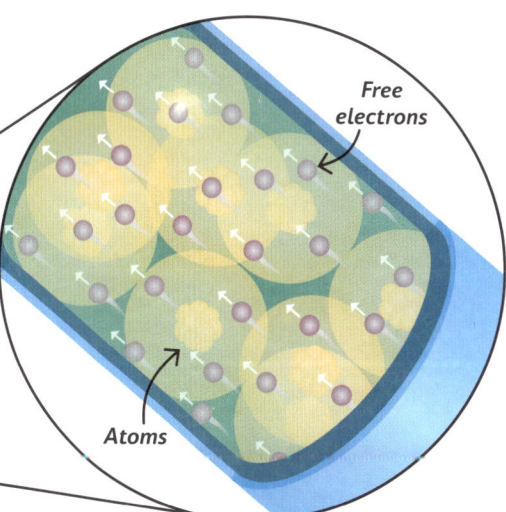

4 Inside the wire, the current is carried by the free electrons. They pass on the charge like a very high-speed relay race

Free electrons

Atoms

Static snake

Use the power of static electricity to make this snake charming trick! It demonstrates electrical attraction in action.

SUPPLIES
metal plate or biscuit tin lid • nylon or silk scarf • plastic ruler • tissue paper scissors • pencil • coloured pens

WHAT TO DO
1. Cut out a disk of tissue paper about 20 cm across. Draw a spiral on it with lines about 2 cm apart.

2. Draw snake-like markings on the spiral with eyes at the centre end. Cut it out.

3. Lay the tissue paper snake on the metal plate then rub the ruler really vigorously with the scarf.

4. Hold the ruler over the snake's head and slowly lift. The snake should spiral up. If it doesn't work at first, you may need to rub the ruler for longer.

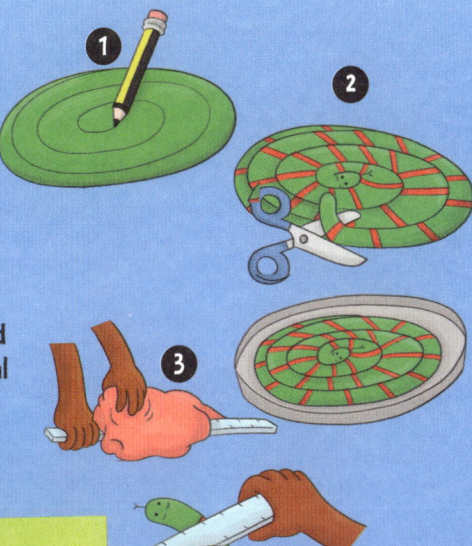

HOW IT WORKS
When you rub the ruler, electrons are knocked off the scarf and onto the ruler, making it negatively charged. It's this charge that draws the snake up.

35

Magnetize!

Magnetism is the invisible force of attraction or repulsion between magnetic materials such as iron. Each magnet has an area around it in which it exerts its force, called its magnetic field. The field gets weaker further from the magnet.

THE POWER OF POLES
Magnetic force is especially strong at the ends of a magnet – the poles. One is called the north pole because if the magnet is suspended freely it swings to point north. The other is the south pole. If opposite poles come together, they attract; if like poles come together, they repel.

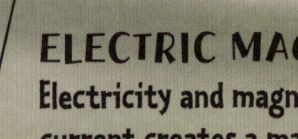

▼ Maglev trains have no wheels but float along the track electromagnetically.

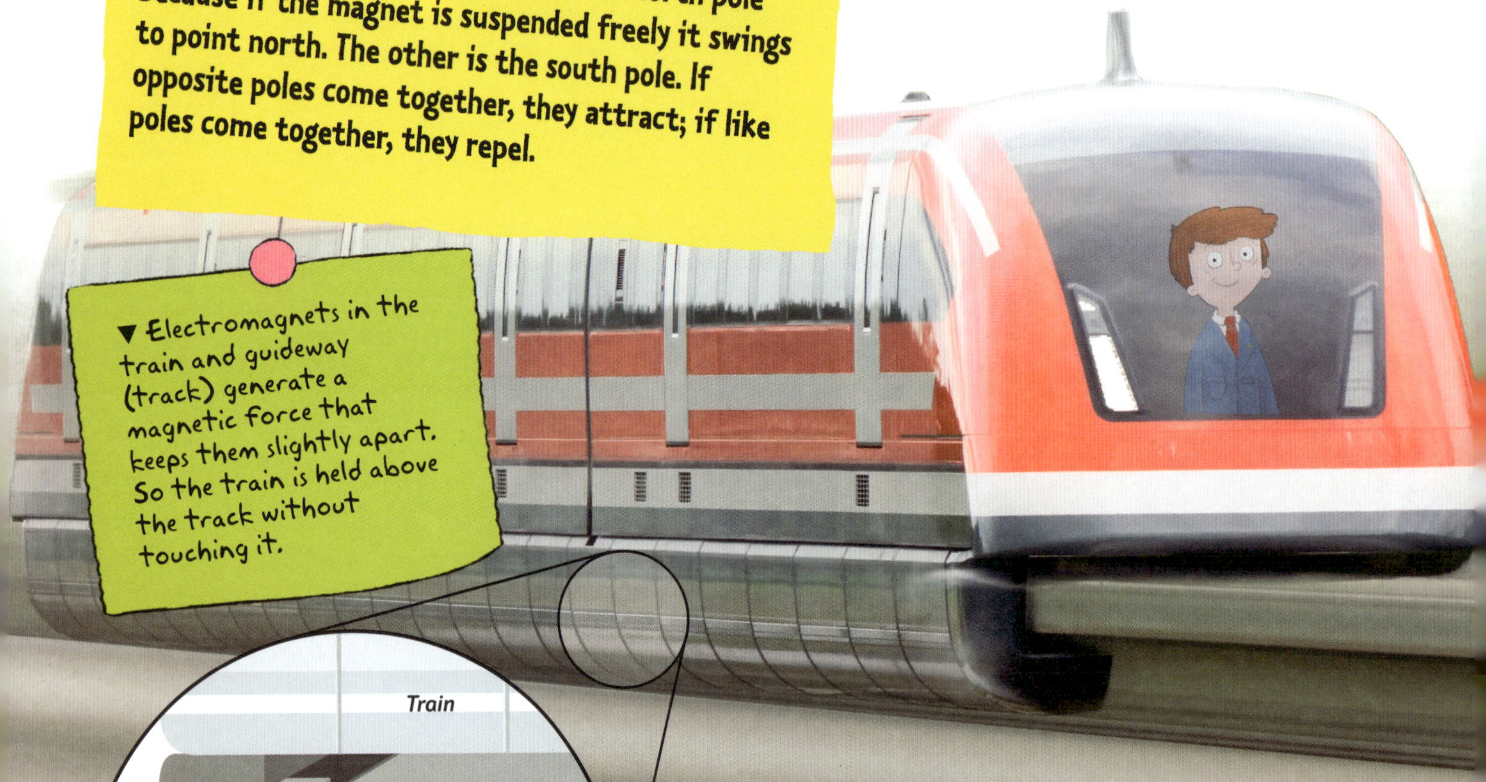

▼ Electromagnets in the train and guideway (track) generate a magnetic force that keeps them slightly apart. So the train is held above the track without touching it.

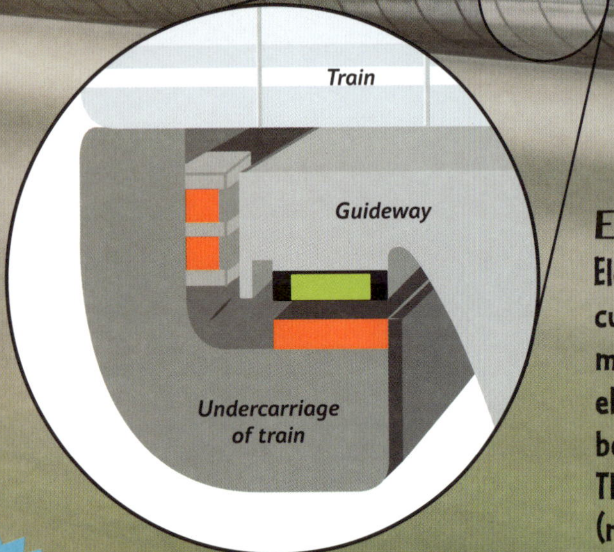

ELECTRIC MAGNETS
Electricity and magnetism are deeply linked. Every electric current creates a magnetic field around it, and moving a magnet past an electric wire generates a current in it. An electromagnet is a coil of wire with an iron core that becomes a strong magnet when the current is switched on. This is the basis for super-fast trains called maglevs (magnetic levitation), which run without any wheels.

Make a compass

A compass is a device that uses a magnet to show the direction of Earth's North Pole. Here you can learn how to make your own!

SUPPLIES
bar magnet • large sewing needle
plastic bowl • cork coaster

HOW TO MAKE
1. Magnetize the needle by stroking it with the magnet 20 times in the same direction. Do this in a looping motion, lifting the magnet away between each stroke.

2. Half-fill the bowl with water, then carefully float the cork coaster as near to the centre as possible.

3. Lay the magnetized needle carefully on the cork, as close to the centre as you can. This makes a simple compass, and the needle should turn to point north.

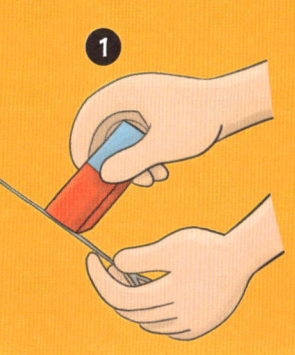

SKY LIGHTS

Sometimes the sky near Earth's poles is filled with glowing lights called aurorae. These are created by charged particles streaming from the Sun. They are pulled into Earth's magnetic field near the poles, where they collide with atoms in the atmosphere. These collisions make bursts of light energy.

▶ Aurorae appear in the sky as dancing curtains of brilliantly coloured light.

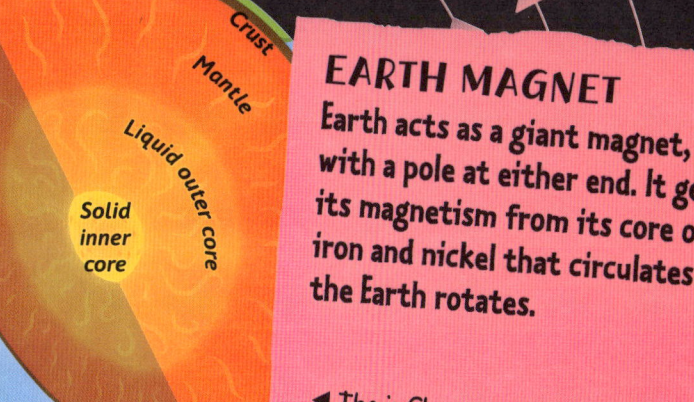

EARTH MAGNET

Earth acts as a giant magnet, with a pole at either end. It gets its magnetism from its core of iron and nickel that circulates as the Earth rotates.

◀ The influence of Earth's magnetic field stretches far out into space, a region called the magnetosphere.

Lighten up

We see things by light. It is radiation emitted by atoms, coming from sources such as the Sun, other stars and electric lights. There are other kinds of radiation, but only light is visible. It always travels in straight lines so people talk about light rays, but rays are really the path light takes.

WHAT IS LIGHT?
It is best to think of light as vibrating packets of energy. Light energy is emitted as tiny particles called photons. A beam of light is made of millions of photons. The colour varies according to the wavelength, or the vibration pattern, of the photons.

▼ A glass wedge or prism bends normal white light so that it splits apart to reveal all the colours it contains. This rainbow is called a spectrum.

White light

Prism

RAINBOW COLOURS
All the colours in a rainbow are different wavelengths of light. Mixed together, the colours blend into white light, which is what the light from the Sun is. But you can split them apart by refracting them (bending at an angle) through a prism to create a spectrum, or through raindrops to create a rainbow.

▼ Each colour is made by light with a different wavelength. The longest waves are red, the shortest are violet.

FAST AS LIGHT
Light is the fastest thing in the Universe. In space, it travels at 299,792,458 m/s, and can travel from the Sun to the Earth in 8 minutes. It travels slightly slower in air, and slower still in water.

Red   Orange   Yellow   Green   Blue

REFLECTION OR REFRACTION?

When light rays hit a surface, some are reflected – they bounce off (1). If the surface is transparent, some light passes through (2). If the rays strike at an angle, they may be refracted (3), because they change speed when passing from one substance to another.

1 When light rays hit a mirror, almost all of the light is reflected.

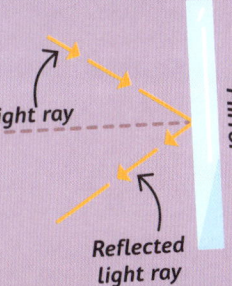

2 When light rays strike a transparent surface at a right angle (90°), they pass straight through.

3 If light rays strike the surface at an angle other than 90°, they are refracted.

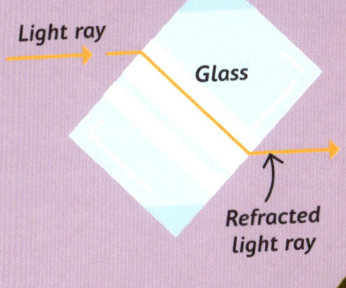

Build a periscope

Light travels in straight lines – but mirrors can make it change direction. You can see this for yourself by making a simple periscope to let you see round corners!

SUPPLIES
cereal box • two small square mirrors • masking tape • glue ruler • pencil • scissors paints and paintbrush

HOW TO MAKE

1. Cut the cereal box so you're left with only the front or back. Copy the template onto the inside. The four columns should each be the same width as the mirrors. The flaps at the ends need to be the same size as the mirrors – measure to make sure.

2. Cut out the template along the solid lines. Using the scissors and ruler, carefully score along all the dotted lines.

3. Fold along each scored line and bend into a box shape. Put glue on the tabs and stick the tabs to the sides. Secure with masking tape if needed. Stick down the flaps.

4. Put glue on the backs of the mirrors and stick one in each of the openings.

5. Paint your periscope. Once it's dry, you can use it to look over walls and round corners!

Make sure these flaps are the same size as the mirrors

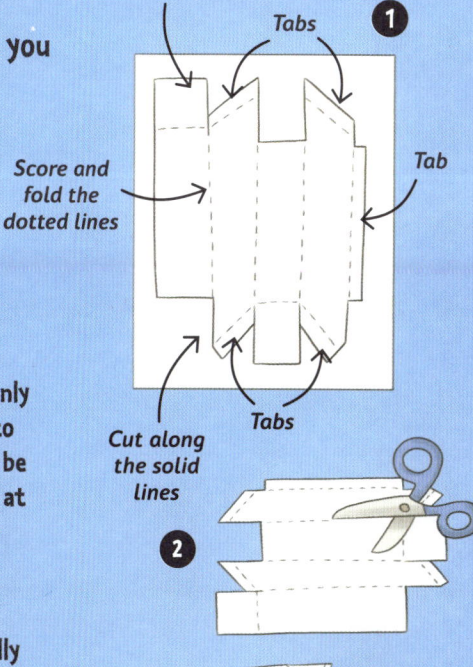

Score and fold the dotted lines

Cut along the solid lines

Indigo   Violet

Sounding out

When anything makes a sound, it sends out vibrations, or sound waves, that squeeze then stretch the air (or water). Sound waves cannot travel through a vacuum such as space because there is nothing to transmit them.

SEARCH AND FIND
To locate its prey, a dolphin sends out high-pitched clicks by pushing air between phonic lips. The melon, a fluid-filled area in its forehead, focuses the sound waves made by the clicks so they travel out from the front of the head in a narrow beam.

ECHOLOCATION
To locate things in the dark or underwater, creatures such as bats and dolphins emit high-pitched squeaks. When the sound hits something, it bounces back as an echo. From the echo, the animal can tell where the object is, as well as its size and shape.

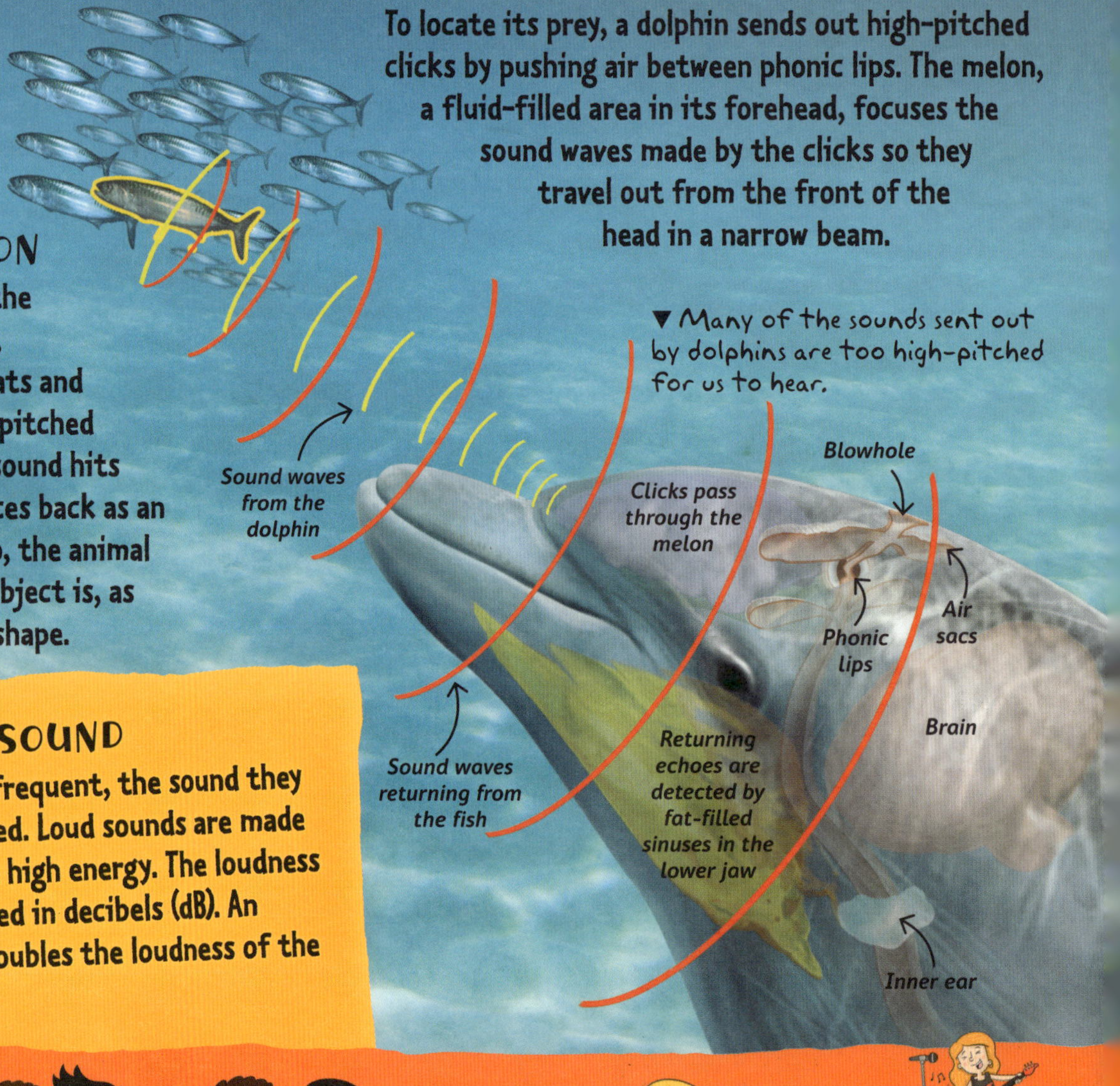

Sound waves from the dolphin

▼ Many of the sounds sent out by dolphins are too high-pitched for us to hear.

Blowhole
Clicks pass through the melon
Phonic lips
Air sacs
Brain
Sound waves returning from the fish
Returning echoes are detected by fat-filled sinuses in the lower jaw
Inner ear

MEASURING SOUND
If sound waves are frequent, the sound they make is high-pitched. Loud sounds are made when the waves are high energy. The loudness of sound is measured in decibels (dB). An increase of 10 dB doubles the loudness of the sound you hear.

dB 0 10 20 30 40 50 60 70 80 90 100 110 120 13
       Pin   Whisper   Normal   Hairdryer   Rock   Firew
       dropping   conversation   concert

Leaves rustling   Passing car

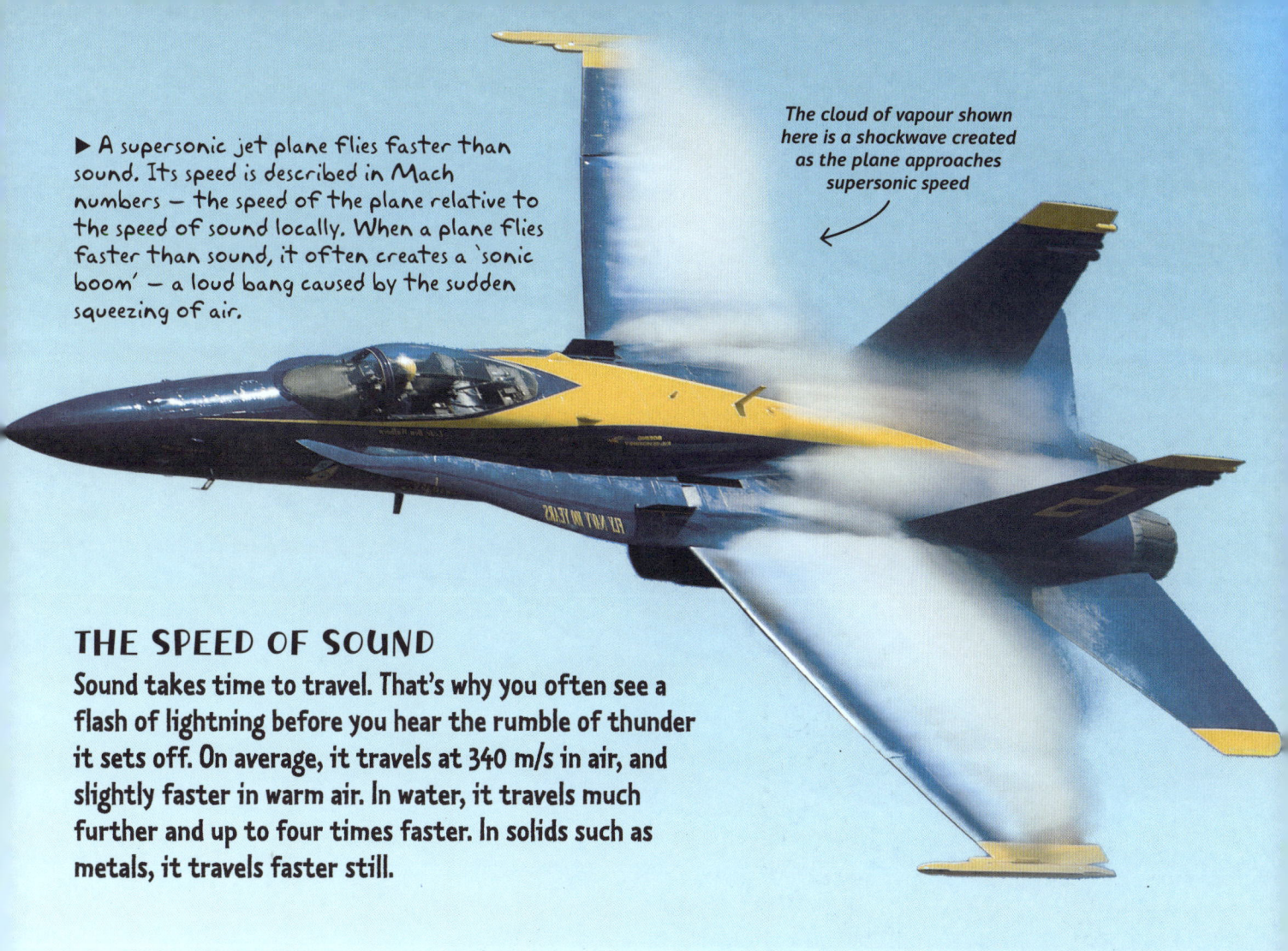

▶ A supersonic jet plane flies faster than sound. Its speed is described in Mach numbers — the speed of the plane relative to the speed of sound locally. When a plane flies faster than sound, it often creates a 'sonic boom' — a loud bang caused by the sudden squeezing of air.

The cloud of vapour shown here is a shockwave created as the plane approaches supersonic speed

THE SPEED OF SOUND

Sound takes time to travel. That's why you often see a flash of lightning before you hear the rumble of thunder it sets off. On average, it travels at 340 m/s in air, and slightly faster in warm air. In water, it travels much further and up to four times faster. In solids such as metals, it travels faster still.

Water music

Learn about pitch and make music at the same time!

SUPPLIES
six strong tall drinking glasses or identical glass bottles • water • thick chopstick piano or keyboard (an online one will do)

WHAT TO DO
1. Fill each glass with a different amount of water. Try to make the differences fairly even.

2. Tap each glass gently with the chopstick. Do they make different-pitched sounds? Which glass makes the highest sound and which the lowest?

3. You will see that the less water there is in the glass, the higher the note (higher pitch). Try adding a little water to the glass or taking it away until they match the pitch of keys on the piano.

4. You now have your own water xylophone. Play some music!

HOW IT WORKS
The glass passes on the vibrations of the stick hitting it to the water. The shorter the column of water, the higher the pitch as the sound waves are higher frequency. So the glass with the most water produces the lowest sound.

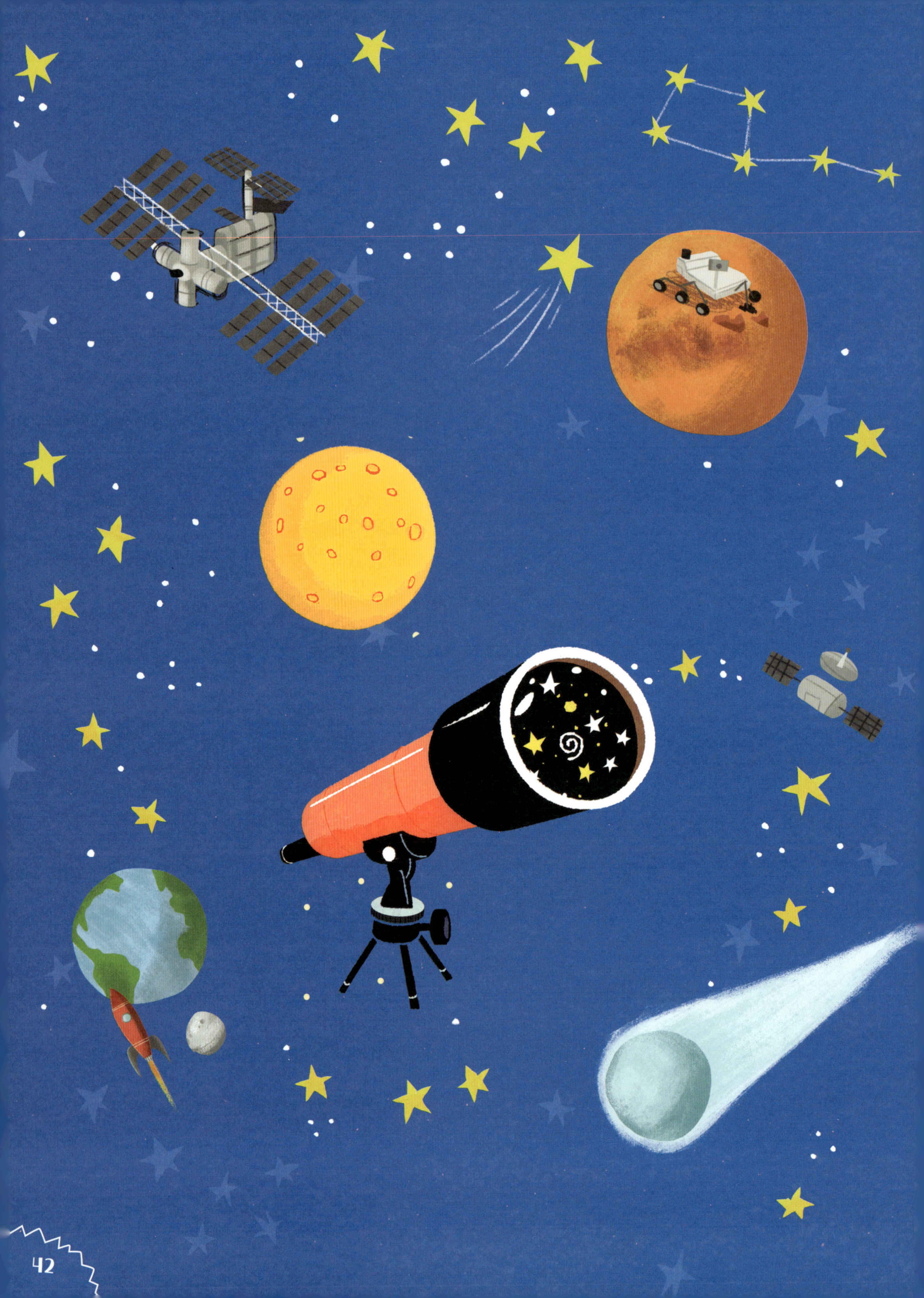

Space

What is space?

When you look up into the clear, dark sky after the Sun has gone down, you're looking at space. Space is the blackness of the night sky – the vast gaps between the stars and planets – and there's lots of it!

IS SPACE EMPTY?
Space looks as if it is completely empty, but it isn't empty at all. Particles of gas and grains of dust whiz about in space all the time, but they're so small and spread out so thinly that you can't see them. Even astronauts in space can't see them.

If you could drive a car straight upwards, you could reach **space in less than an hour!**

▶ A telescope looks out into space from a mountain-top above the clouds on the island of La Palma in the Canary Islands.

WHAT CAN YOU SEE IN SPACE?

The biggest, brightest thing in the night sky is the Moon. It moves through space with Earth, and they are 384,400 km apart. They're held together by an invisible force called gravity, which also holds you down on the ground!

▶ The Moon's centre is a ball of solid iron 480 km across. This is surrounded by liquid metal. The rest (the mantle and crust) is rock.

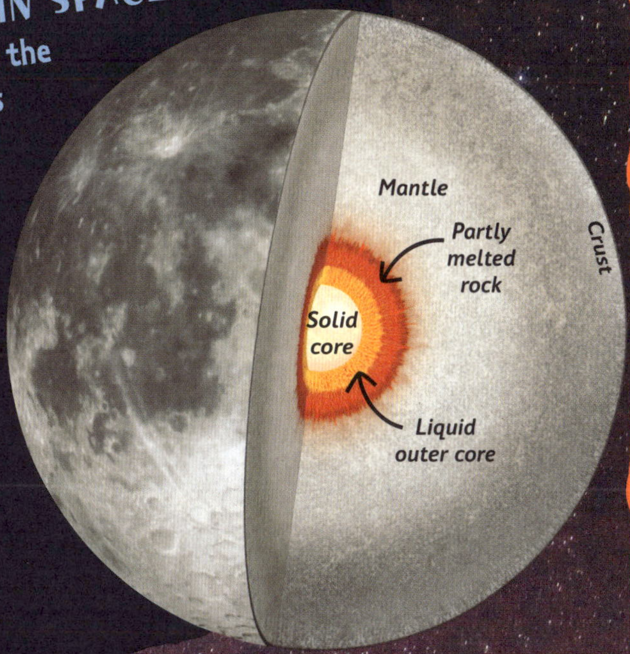

Mantle
Partly melted rock
Crust
Solid core
Liquid outer core

Where does space begin?

Space isn't very far away. It begins about **100 km** above your head. At this height, there is almost no air at all.

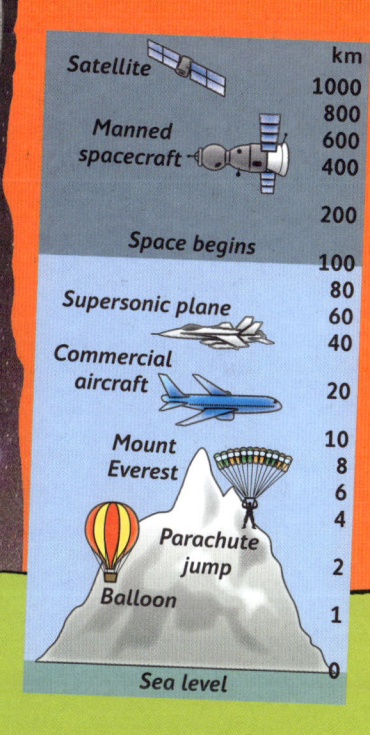

	km
Satellite	1000
	800
Manned spacecraft	600
	400
	200
Space begins	100
	80
Supersonic plane	60
	40
Commercial aircraft	20
	10
Mount Everest	8
	6
	4
Parachute jump	2
Balloon	1
Sea level	0

Paper moon

You can make your own moon from a balloon and strips of newspaper.

SUPPLIES
newspaper • round balloon • PVA glue • bowl
water-based black and white paint • paintbrush

HOW TO MAKE

1. Tear the newspaper into strips.

2. Blow up the balloon until it is a small, round shape and tie a knot in its neck.

3. Put some PVA glue into a bowl.

4. Dip a strip of newspaper into the glue and lay it on the balloon. Add more glued strips, overlapping them until the whole balloon is covered. Build up thicker layers in some places to make mountains.

5. When the glue is dry, you can paint your moon. Mix the black and white paint to make shades of grey. Add shadowy craters just like the real Moon.

HOW TO USE
Look at your moon and see how it compares to the real thing.

Big Bang!

Where do the stars and planets come from? Scientists think that everything was once a tiny speck, thousands of times smaller than a pinhead! The speck burst out in a huge explosion called the Big Bang. It was the birth of everything.

The first atoms

The first particles

2 A fraction of a second after the Big Bang, the Universe cooled down enough for some of its energy to change into the first particles.

1 The Universe created by the Big Bang was a super-hot fireball. It started small, but grew bigger, and it cooled as it grew.

3 After three more minutes, the Universe had cooled to less than one billion degrees Celsius — cool enough for the particles to start joining together, forming more complex particles.

Timeline

Time	Big Bang	Less than one second	Three minutes
Temperature	Billions of degrees Celsius	More than one billion degrees Celsius	Less than one billion degrees Celsius

46

STILL GROWING
The Universe has been growing bigger ever since the Big Bang. It's still growing today. Scientists can see distant parts of the Universe rushing away from us. It will carry on growing for a long time. No one knows if it will ever stop growing.

The first stars

6 As the first stars came and went, they spread gas and dust through space. This formed the stars and planets we see today.

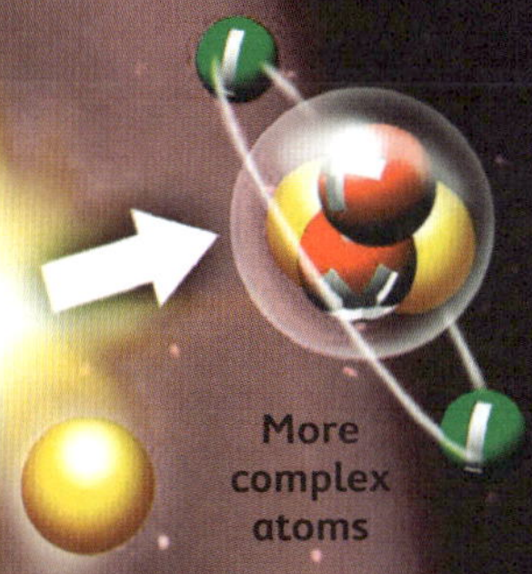

The planets we see today

4 When the Universe was 300,000 years old, it had cooled enough for the first atoms to form. Atoms are the building blocks of everything you can see.

5 The Universe was filled with clouds of gas, mostly hydrogen and helium. One billion years after the Big Bang, gravity started pulling clumps of gas together — they became the first stars.

Puffed-up universe
You can see how the expanding Universe makes everything move further apart by making your own from a balloon.

SUPPLIES
round balloon • black permanent marker
ruler

HOW TO MAKE
1. Draw two black dots on the balloon. Use the ruler to space them about one centimetre apart.

2. Blow up the balloon and tie a knot in its neck.

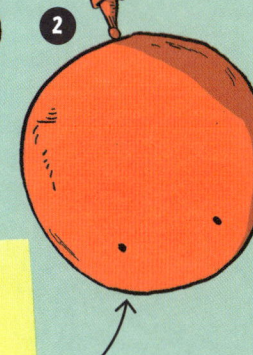

More complex atoms

Long ago, people thought the **Universe** was powered by a giant **machine!**

HOW TO USE
Measure how far apart the dots are. They are now further than one centimetre apart. As the Universe expands, parts of it move further apart.

300,000 years	One billion years	13.8 billion years (current age of the Universe)
10,000°C	-200°C	-270°C (current temperature of the Universe)

47

Super sizzlers

The night sky is full of thousands of stars. The Sun is a star. Some stars are bigger than our Sun, others are smaller. They look like tiny points of light because they are much further away from us than our Sun.

STAR BRIGHT

Why do you think stars are so bright? They look as if they're burning, but they don't burn like a flame. Stars are more like nuclear power stations in space. Their heat and light come from particles of matter smashing into each other in the centre of each star. This is called nuclear fusion.

▶ The Pleiades cluster is a group of hot blue stars. The haze around them is dust lit up by the stars.

RED GIANT

When a star forms (1) it shines brightly. A star like the Sun shines for billions of years (2). When it runs out of fuel, it swells up and cools down (3). As it cools, it becomes a red giant star (4). Then it pushes most of its gas away into space, leaving a tiny fading star called a white dwarf (5).

When the Sun turns into a red giant, it might grow big enough to **swallow** the Earth, but not for another **five billion** years!

munch munch

GOING TO PIECES

When stars bigger than the Sun grow into red giants, they blow themselves to bits in a cosmic explosion called a supernova. This sends all the elements made by the star flying out into space.

▶ After the explosion, the star collapses and forms a strange dark star, called a neutron star.

Supernova

Cool stars

Stars are different **colours**. Scientists can tell how hot a star is from its colour. The Sun is a yellow star.

Hottest
Blue star
11,000–28,000°C

White star
7500–11,000°C

Yellow star
5000–6000°C

Orange star
3600–5000°C

Red star
2000–3600°C
Coolest

Twinkle, twinkle, little star

Stars twinkle because starlight bends and twists as it travels through the air around Earth. You can see this happening by making your own stars and making them twinkle.

SUPPLIES
glass bowl • cardboard (from a cereal box) • scissors
pen • aluminium foil • torch

HOW TO MAKE
1. Pour cold water into the bowl until it's about two-thirds full.

2. Cut out a piece of cardboard bigger than the base of the bowl.

3. Draw small star shapes on the aluminium foil. Cut them out.

4. Place the stars on top of the cardboard and then place the bowl on top of the stars.

HOW TO USE
Close the curtains to darken the room and switch on the torch. Point the torch down into the bowl. Now tap the bowl and see the stars twinkle. The light from the torch is bent as it passes through the rippling water, in the same way as starlight is bent as it passes through the air around Earth.

49

Star cities

Stars travel through space with other stars. They huddle together in galaxies. Each galaxy has billions of stars and there are billions of galaxies. Most galaxies are so far away that you need a telescope to see them.

Too cool!

The biggest galaxies have one **trillion** (1000 billion) stars.

Stars and **galaxies** are so far apart that the distances between them are measured in **light years**.

A light year is the distance light travels in a year.

The smallest galaxies have fewer than one **billion** (1000 million) stars.

Elliptical galaxy

Elliptical galaxies are the shape of a ball, or a ball that's been squashed. Some have such a squashed shape that they look long and thin.

Irregular galaxies have all sorts of different shapes. They may have been formed by collisions and near misses between different galaxies.

Irregular galaxy

50

Spiral galaxy

Spiral galaxies have long arms of stars curling out from a big ball of stars at the centre. About three-quarters of all galaxies are spirals.

CRASH COURSE

It can take billions of years, but galaxies sometimes crash into each other. When two galaxies meet, long streams of stars are sent flying away. The two galaxies might stay together to form a new galaxy, or part and go their separate ways.

▼ These colliding galaxies are called the Mice Galaxies because of their long tails of stars.

Galactic art

Galaxies travel through space together in groups. We travel in a group of about 50 galaxies. Make your own group of galaxies!

SUPPLIES
plastic sheet (or bin liner) • coffee filters • water-based marker pens • eye dropper (or drinking straw) • cup of water • glue stick • glitter • scissors • large sheet of black paper

HOW TO MAKE
1. Lay the plastic sheet on the floor or a table and place the coffee filters on top of it.

2. Use the water-based marker pens to draw galaxies of stars on the coffee filters. Draw spirals, ellipses (squashed circles) and odd shapes, and make them different sizes.

3. Use the eye-dropper to drip water from the cup onto the coffee filters, making the colours run together. Leave the filters to dry.

4. Spread glue over your galaxies and sprinkle glitter on top. Leave to dry, then cut them out. Stick your galaxies to the black paper.

HOW TO USE
Display your colourful group of galaxies poster on your wall.

Gas and dust

Stars aren't the only things in galaxies. There are clouds of gas and dust too, called nebulae. Some of this gas and dust is all that remains of old stars. The matter you are made of came from stars too – you are made of stardust!

COOL!

LIGHT AND DARK
Some nebulae glow because they are heated or lit up by nearby stars. Hot hydrogen gas in a nebula glows pink. Starlight reflected by a nebula looks blue. Some parts of a nebula are as dark as night, because thick dust blocks the light from glowing stars and gas behind them.

▶ New stars are forming inside these vast pillars of gas and dust in the Eagle Nebula.

HOT AND COLD
The Boomerang Nebula is the coldest place in the Universe — a teeth-chattering −272°C. The Tarantula Nebula is one of the hottest — stars heat it to more than one million degrees.

▶ The Boomerang Nebula is made of gas rushing away from a central star.

COSMIC CRAB

Some nebulae are made by exploding stars. The explosion throws gas and dust out in all directions, sometimes in strange and beautiful patterns. These nebulae are often named after whatever they look like.

▼ The Crab Nebula was caused by a star explosion nearly 1000 years ago. Someone looking at it through a telescope thought it looked like a crab!

Star nurseries

Stars are born in **nebulae**. It takes about ten million years to make a star.

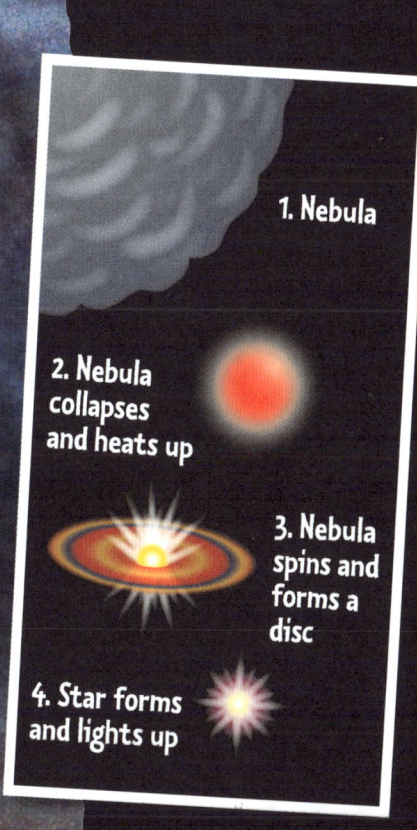

1. Nebula

2. Nebula collapses and heats up

3. Nebula spins and forms a disc

4. Star forms and lights up

Looking for nebulae

Some nebulae are big enough and bright enough to see without a telescope. You just have to know where to look.

WHAT TO DO
Look for the constellation (group of stars) called Orion. If you live in the northern half of Earth, Orion appears in the night sky during the autumn and winter. If you live in the southern half of Earth, it appears in the spring and summer. It looks like this.

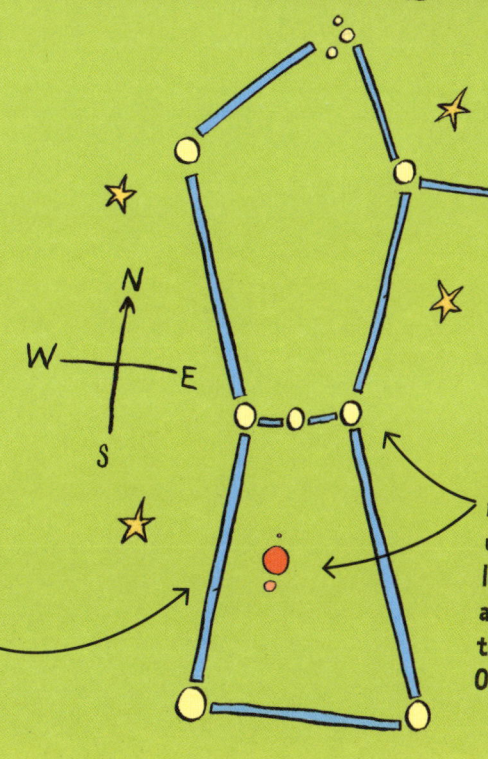

Look for three bright stars across the middle (Orion's Belt). If you live in the northern half of Earth, look downwards until you come to something that looks like a fuzzy star. It isn't a star at all — it's the Orion Nebula. If you live in the southern half of Earth, you'll see Orion the other way up.

53

Greedy galaxy

The galaxy we live in is called the Milky Way. It's a spiral galaxy, with arms of stars and nebulae curling out from a bulging centre. It is thought that the Milky Way may have built itself up by swallowing other, smaller galaxies.

Our galaxy

The Milky Way formed about **12 billion** years ago, just 1-2 billion years after the **Big Bang**.

The Milky Way moves through space at the incredible speed of **2.2 million** km/h!

Our galaxy is spinning. The Sun makes one lap every **230 million** years!

1 If aliens from a faraway galaxy arrived at the edge of the Milky Way, they would find a vast disc of stars and dust clouds.

2 Moving towards the centre of the galaxy, the aliens would travel through arms of stars in the shape of a flattened disc.

3 As the aliens neared the centre of the Milky Way, they would find a big bulging ball of stars. These are mainly older stars.

6 Scientists think a gigantic, matter-gobbling black hole is at the centre of the Milky Way. The aliens might have to be careful to avoid being sucked in!

5 The bulge of stars hides the centre of the galaxy. What do you think the aliens will find when they get there?

4 As the aliens circled the galaxy, they might notice a star with eight planets going around it — our Solar System.

PATHWAY IN THE SKY

The dusty, gassy spiral arms of our galaxy look like a hazy band of light stretching across the night sky. People in the ancient world didn't know what this strange sight was, but their myths and legends tried to explain it. The ancient Greeks thought it was a trail of milk spilt by a goddess called Hera.

▶ If you look up into a clear sky in a very dark place, especially between June and September, you might see the Milky Way.

55

The Sun's family

The Solar System is made up of the eight planets, their moons and all the smaller objects that circle the Sun. Some of the planets are small and rocky, others are huge and gassy – but they are all part of Earth's family in space.

WOWZERS!

If you were a **space traveller**, you would see **awesome** features to write home about.

▼ The enormous extinct volcano, Olympus Mons, on Mars is a must-see. It's three times taller than Mount Everest – the tallest mountain on Earth!

▶ It takes a spacecraft at least five months to reach Sun-scorched Mercury from Earth, but the sight of its crater-scarred surface is worth the journey.

Mercury Venus Earth The Moon Mars

You are here

If the Sun was the size of a **bowling ball**, the Solar System would be just **1.6 km** across!

◀ Venus' choking atmosphere hides its surface from view, so you have to go below the clouds to see its hostile landscape of volcanoes, valleys and weird lava formations.

WANDERING PLANETS

The planets in the Solar System seem to wander around the sky. They orbit the Sun at different speeds. Earth travels through space on its endless journey around the Sun more than twice as fast as Jupiter and nearly six times faster than Neptune.

▶ The ancient Greeks came up with the word planet, meaning wanderer, for these objects, which they thought looked like wandering stars in the sky.

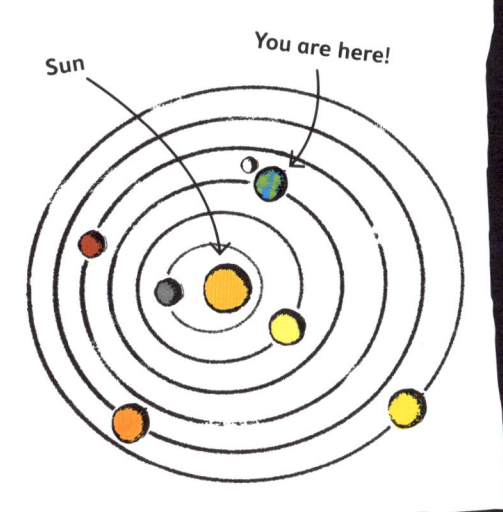

Sun

You are here!

Turn the page to see the rest of the planets in our Solar System

Asteroid belt

Jupiter

Millions of weird-shaped rocks called **asteroids** can be found between Mars and Jupiter.

Jupiter's biggest moons

Ganymede is the Solar System's **largest** moon and is **bigger** than Mercury.

▶ Jupiter's four biggest moons are called the Galilean moons, because they were discovered in 1610 by the Italian astronomer, Galileo Galilei.

Io
Europa
Ganymede
Callisto

57

Further away

If you explore the Solar System and zoom out past Jupiter, you'll find three more planets. They are all much bigger than Earth – but Jupiter is bigger than all the other planets combined.

Uranus' biggest moons

▲ The incredible ice geysers on Saturn's moon, Enceladus, are rare in the Solar System. No expedition to the planets would be complete without a snapshot!

If there was a **bathtub** big enough to hold **Saturn** it would float in the water!

Saturn

Saturn's biggest moons

HOW MANY MOONS?
Generally, the bigger the planet, the more moons it has. Jupiter, the biggest planet, with the strongest gravity, has the most.

Mercury	Venus	Earth	Mars	Jupiter	Saturn	Uranus	Neptune
0	0	1	2	64	62	27	13

▶ Neptune's gassy surface is streaked with raging storms and bands of clouds. Its freezing conditions make it a desolate place, so you won't want to linger for long.

Uranus

Heat and pressure inside **Neptune** change methane gas into **diamonds!**

Neptune

Neptune's biggest moons

◀ One of Uranus' moons, Miranda, has a fascinating surface, with giant canyons as much as 12 times as deep as the Grand Canyon on Earth!

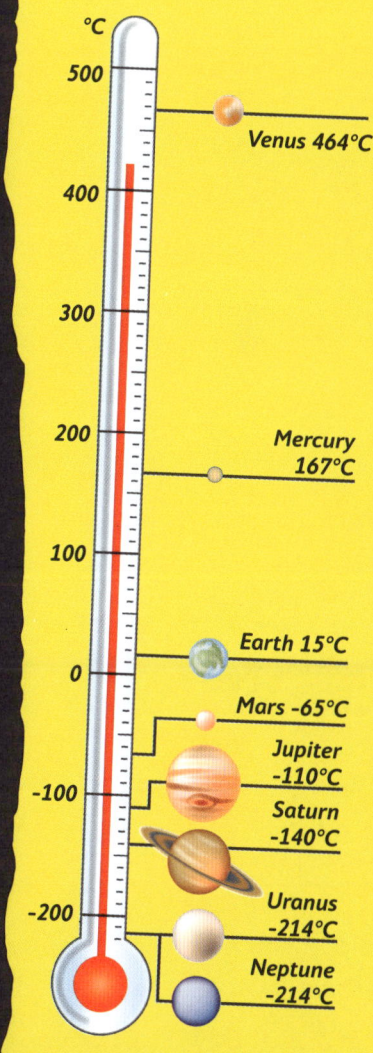

Uranus rolls around on its side, giving it weird seasons. Each pole has 42 years of continuous **daylight**, then 42 years of **night!**

TINY PLANETS
In 2006 astronomers decided that Pluto is too small and its orbit is too unusual for it to be called a planet. They decided to call it a dwarf planet.

▶ Another dwarf planet, called Eris, was discovered in 2005.

Cool Planets

Planets closer to the **Sun**, such as Mercury and Venus, are **hotter** than those further out, like **freezing** cold Neptune.

°C
500 — Venus 464°C
400
300
200 — Mercury 167°C
100
0 — Earth 15°C
— Mars -65°C
— Jupiter -110°C
-100 — Saturn -140°C
-200 — Uranus -214°C
— Neptune -214°C

59

Super star

Our star, the Sun, is a giant ball of fiery, glowing gas. It provides the heat and light that sustains life on Earth. The Sun is vital to us, but it is only one of about 200 billion stars in our galaxy.

Sunspots are slightly cooler areas on the Sun's surface

Solar flares look like huge flames shooting out from the Sun's surface

INSIDE THE SUN

The Sun's core is the source of its energy. Particles of matter in the core give out energy which travels outwards to the surface through a series of zones. The radiative zone radiates the energy away from the core. Bubbles of hot gas rising through the convective zone carry the energy to the photosphere, where it escapes into space.

◀ Energy can take more than 100,000 years to travel to the Sun's surface. Then it takes just over eight minutes to reach Earth.

Core

Radiative zone

Convective zone

Photosphere

TOTAL ECLIPSE

Sometimes the Sun, Moon and Earth line up. As the Moon passes between the Sun and Earth, the Moon's shadow falls on Earth. This is called a solar eclipse. If you are in the darkest part of the shadow, you will see a total eclipse. In the partial shadow around this, you will see a partial eclipse.

▼ The Moon passes in front of the Sun during a partial solar eclipse seen from China in May, 2012.

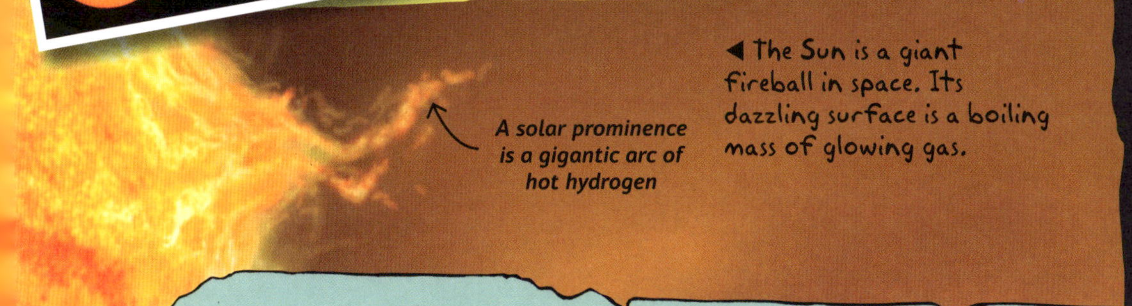

◀ A solar prominence is a gigantic arc of hot hydrogen

◀ The Sun is a giant fireball in space. Its dazzling surface is a boiling mass of glowing gas.

Too cool!

The Sun is 150 million km away from Earth. That's the same as 3700 trips around Earth!

The Sun is so enormous that more than one **million** Earths would fit inside it!

The Sun's surface temperature is about 5700°C. That's more than 250 times hotter than Earth!

Eclipse kit

To see how an eclipse works, you can make this model. You will need to ask an adult for help.

WARNING: Never look at the Sun, especially with binoculars or a telescope. This can seriously damage your eyes or even make you blind.

SUPPLIES
shoebox • scissors • black card • yellow tissue paper • sticky tape • cocktail stick

HOW TO MAKE
1. Cut a window at each end of your shoebox and then cut a slit across the top of the box.

2. Cut out a square of black card small enough to slide into the slit in the box.

3. Cut a circle out of the middle of the card and stick yellow tissue paper over the hole.

4. Stick a cocktail stick to the black card circle (you will use this as your Moon).

5. Slide the square of card into the slit in the box and hold the box up to the light. Look through it to see your Sun.

HOW TO USE
Push your Moon into the slit in the box behind the square of card. Move it slowly across your Sun to make an eclipse.

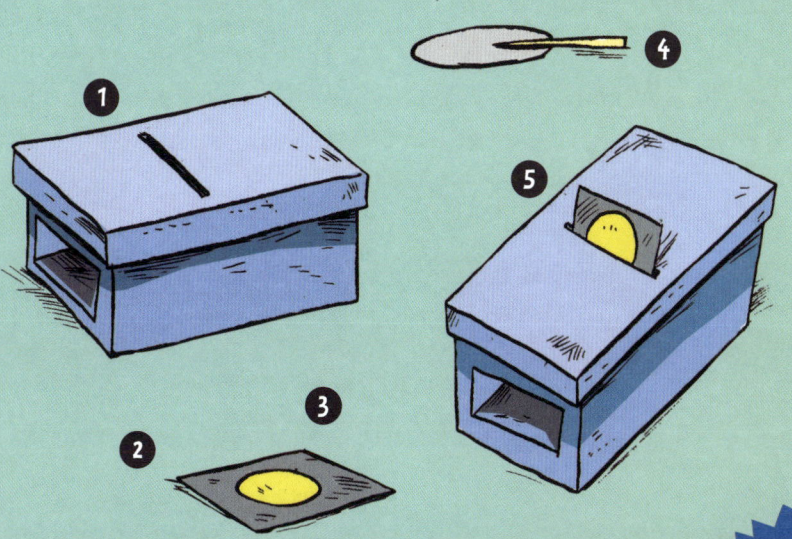

61

Rocky worlds

The four planets closest to the Sun are smaller than the other four planets. They're made of rock and have few moons, or none at all. One of these planets is our home – Earth. We live on the third planet from the Sun.

Spewing volcanoes

All four rocky worlds have **volcanoes**, or had them in the past.

Mars has the biggest volcano in the Solar System – Olympus Mons.

Venus has more volcanoes than any other planet in the Solar System.

HOT STUFF

Mercury is the closest planet to the Sun, but Venus is the hottest planet. It is covered by a blanket of thick clouds that soak up lots of heat from the Sun like a giant greenhouse.

WHERE ARE ALL THE MARTIANS?

In the 1870s, astronomer Giovanni Schiaparelli looked through a telescope at Mars. He thought he saw straight lines on the planet. Astronomer Percival Lowell saw them too. He thought they were canals built by Martians. However, the first spacecraft that visited Mars in the 1960s found no canals or Martians.

▲ These four rocky worlds (not shown in order) are also known as the inner planets, because they are the closest planets to the Sun.

HIDDEN LAYERS

Earth's core (centre) is a big ball of metal, mainly iron. The middle is solid, with liquid metal around it. The core is surrounded by rock called the mantle. We live on the crust, a thin layer of rock on top of the mantle.

▼ If you could slice through Earth and look inside, you would find a series of layers.

Inner core · Outer core · Mantle · Crust

Earth

Exploding volcano

Volcanoes spew out molten rock called lava. You can make your own volcano and see this happening!

SUPPLIES
plastic sheet • earth or damp sand • small bottle • baking soda • washing-up liquid • red and yellow food colouring • vinegar

HOW TO MAKE
1. On a plastic sheet, make your volcano out of earth or damp sand around a small bottle in the middle.

2. Add 3 tablespoons of baking soda and one tablespoon of washing-up liquid to the bottle. Then add a few drops of each food colouring.

HOW TO USE
Pour some vinegar into the bottle and stand back. The vinegar and baking soda will react together, producing lots of carbon dioxide gas, which will make bubbles (helped by the soap), producing a foaming, frothing eruption. The food colouring will colour your erupting lava.

GOLDILOCKS EARTH

Earth is a Goldilocks planet, which means it is not too far from the Sun or too close to it — it's just right for life. If Earth was closer to the Sun, it would be too hot for anything to live here, and if it was further away it would be too cold.

Mercury · Venus · Earth · Mars

Goldilocks Zone

63

Gassy giants

The four planets furthest from the Sun are the biggest planets in the Solar System. You can't land on them because they don't have any solid ground. These huge planets are mostly made of liquid and gas.

Saturn

Jupiter

Hydrogen gas

Liquid hydrogen

Cloud tops

Metallic hydrogen

Rock core

▼ The rocky core is a tiny part of the planet, but it's bigger than Earth!

ICY RINGS
All four of the giant gas planets have rings around them. However, the rings around Jupiter, Uranus and Neptune are thin, dusty and dark, so they're hard to see. Saturn's rings are bright and easy to see because they're made of ice, which is good at reflecting sunlight.

◄► The four gas giants (not shown in order) are different colours because they have different chemicals in their clouds.

INSIDE THE GIANTS
The gas giants look alike inside. A ball of rock in the middle is surrounded by liquid and gas. Jupiter and Saturn are made mainly of hydrogen. Uranus and Neptune are mostly water, methane and ammonia.

GREAT RED SPOT
Look at any close-up photograph of Jupiter and the first thing you notice is a big red oval — this is the Great Red Spot. It's a giant storm that has been rolling around Jupiter for at least 300 years. The Great Red Spot is three times the size of Earth!

Speedy planets

Planets close to the Sun travel through space faster than planets further away. You can see this with a paper planet.

SUPPLIES
newspaper • water-based paint
string • sticky tape

HOW TO MAKE
1. Make a planet from a ball of tightly scrunched-up newspaper. You could even paint your paper planet to look like a real planet — make it stripy like Jupiter or red like Mars.

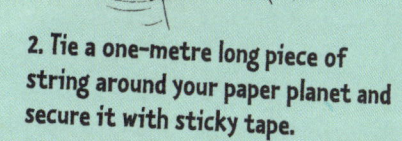

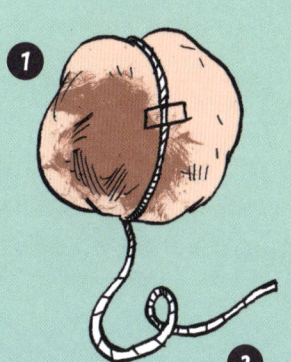

2. Tie a one-metre long piece of string around your paper planet and secure it with sticky tape.

HOW TO USE
In an open space outside, hold the end of the string and swing your planet around above your head. The pull of the string acts like gravity and pulls the planet round into a circular orbit. Now hold the string in the middle. You'll find that you have to swing the planet round faster.

LONG AND SLOW
The gas giants take a long time to go around the Sun. Jupiter takes nearly 12 years, Saturn takes 29 years, Uranus 84 years and Neptune 165 years.

What a gas!

Uranus was the first planet to be discovered by someone using a telescope – William Herschel in **1781**.

Jupiter is made mostly of hydrogen, which stars are made of. If Jupiter had grown ten times bigger, it would have become a **star!**

65

Space rocks

Planets and moons aren't the only things flying around the Solar System. Countless smaller rocks swarm around the Sun too. Most of them are too small and too far away for us to see, even with a telescope, but we know they're there.

At least **1000 tonnes** of space rock falls to Earth every day, most of it no bigger than **dust particles**.

Amazing asteroids!

The smallest asteroids are about the size of a house. The **biggest** are nearly **1000 km** across!

Asteroid Ceres
Discovered 1801
Diameter 952 km

Asteroid Pallas
Discovered 1802
Diameter 544 km

Asteroid Vesta
Discovered 1807
Diameter 525 km

Jupiter

Asteroid belt

▶ Millions of pieces of rock swarm around the Sun in a broad belt between Mars and Jupiter.

FLYING APART

The pieces of rock orbiting the Sun in the asteroid belt might have joined together if it were not for Jupiter. Jupiter's gravity pulls the rocks apart. It also stops most of them from flying closer to the Sun and perhaps hitting Earth. Scientists keep an eye on all the big asteroids in case any of them head our way.

ALIEN ROCKS

Space rocks smaller than asteroids are called meteoroids. They can be as small as a speck of dust or as big as a 10-m boulder. The smallest burn up as shooting stars. Larger ones can reach the ground, at which point they are called meteorites.

▶ This giant crater in Arizona, USA, was made by a meteorite.

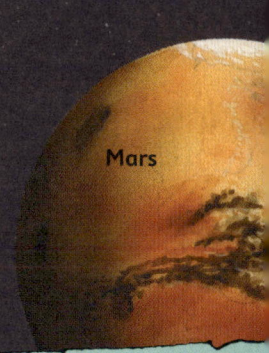

Mars

Space rock hunt

Space rocks fall to Earth every day. They're called meteorites. Most of them are tiny and harmless. You can look for them with a magnet.

SUPPLIES
bucket or bowl • newspaper
magnet • small plastic bag
sheet of white paper
magnifying glass

WHAT TO DO

1. Put a bucket or bowl outside when it rains. If possible, put it under a drain spout from a roof to collect lots of water.

2. When it's full, take out any large twigs and leaves, and then carefully pour away most of the water. You should find some fine, dark, dusty dirt at the bottom.

3. Pour the last few drops of water with the dark particles onto a sheet of newspaper, and set the paper aside indoors until it dries out.

4. Put a magnet inside a small plastic bag and move it slowly back and forth across the paper. Some of the particles may stick to the outside of the bag.

5. Turn the bag inside out and take the magnet away. The dark dust is now inside the bag. Carefully empty the bag onto a sheet of white paper.

HOW TO USE
Have a look at the particles through a magnifying glass. You've collected micrometeorites — tiny rocks from space. Sand, dust and dirt don't stick to a magnet, but rocks from space do, because they contain iron.

KNOBBLY WORLDS

Most asteroids and meteoroids have a knobbly shape. Their tiny pull of gravity isn't strong enough to pull them into a round shape like a planet. Craters on their surface show where other asteroids and meteoroids have crashed into them.

TAKE THAT! NO, TAKE THIS!

Cosmic snowballs

If you look up into the sky one night and see something like a star with a long, bright tail, your eyes aren't playing tricks on you. You're looking at a comet — a mountain of ice and rock orbiting the Sun.

Astronomers saw a **comet** slamming into the planet **Jupiter** in 1994.

Nucleus
Coma
Gas tail
Dust tail

◀ A comet's tails can be as long as 160 million km.

INSIDE A COMET
A comet has tails only when it is close to the Sun. The Sun's warmth changes some of the comet's dusty ice to gas. The gas and dust form a coma (a big hazy ball) around the comet's head. Some of this dust and gas forms the comet's tails.

TELLING TAILS
A comet's tails always point away from the Sun. Gas and dust around a comet's head are stretched out into tails by sunlight and a stream of particles given out by the Sun, called the solar wind — so the tails are always pushed away from the Sun.

◀ As a comet nears the Sun, its tails grow longer and brighter.

ICE WORLDS
The Solar System is surrounded by millions of comets. If you could travel past Neptune, you'd find a swarm of comets and icy worlds called the Kuiper Belt, which includes the dwarf planet Pluto. Even further away, there is another swarm of comets called the Oort Cloud.

BAD LUCK
In 1066, a comet appeared just as soldiers were gathering to fight the Battle of Hastings in England. When King Harold of England saw it, he thought it was a sign of bad luck. He then lost the battle!

Famous comets
Halley's Comet has been returning every 76 years for at least 2250 years. Look out for it in 2061!

In 1770, Lexell's Comet came closer to Earth than any other comet. It looked as big as the Moon.

The brightest comet ever seen appeared in 1882. It was brighter than the Moon and could be seen in daylight.

A tale of tails
A comet grows brighter the closer it is to the Sun. See this happening by making your own comet.

SUPPLIES
black card • scissors • coloured pencils or crayons (black and yellow) • hole punch (or sharp pencil) • split pin

HOW TO MAKE
1. Cut out a square of black card and draw an ellipse (a stretched circle) on it. Draw a bright yellow sun near one end of the ellipse.

2. Use the hole punch to make holes about one centimetre apart all along the line of your ellipse. Or you can push a sharp pencil through the card to make the holes. Make sure you can see through the holes.

3. Take another sheet of black card and cut out a circle bigger than the square. Draw a bright yellow strip from the centre to the edge. Make the part near the centre the brightest and then make the yellow colour fade out towards the edge.

4. Place the card with the Sun on it on top of the other piece of card. Push a split pin through the Sun and the centre of the other sheet to hold the two sheets together.

HOW TO USE
Hold the top card still and slowly turn the bottom sheet. You'll see your comet grow brighter as it comes closer to the Sun, with its tail pointing away from the Sun, just like a real comet.

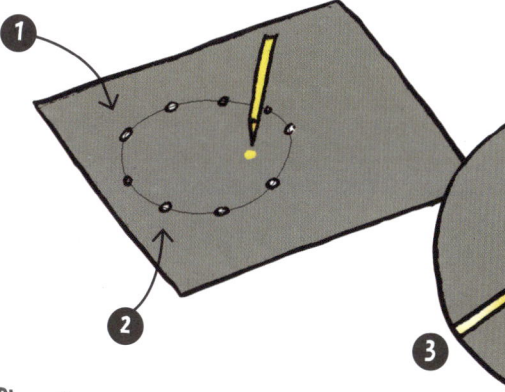

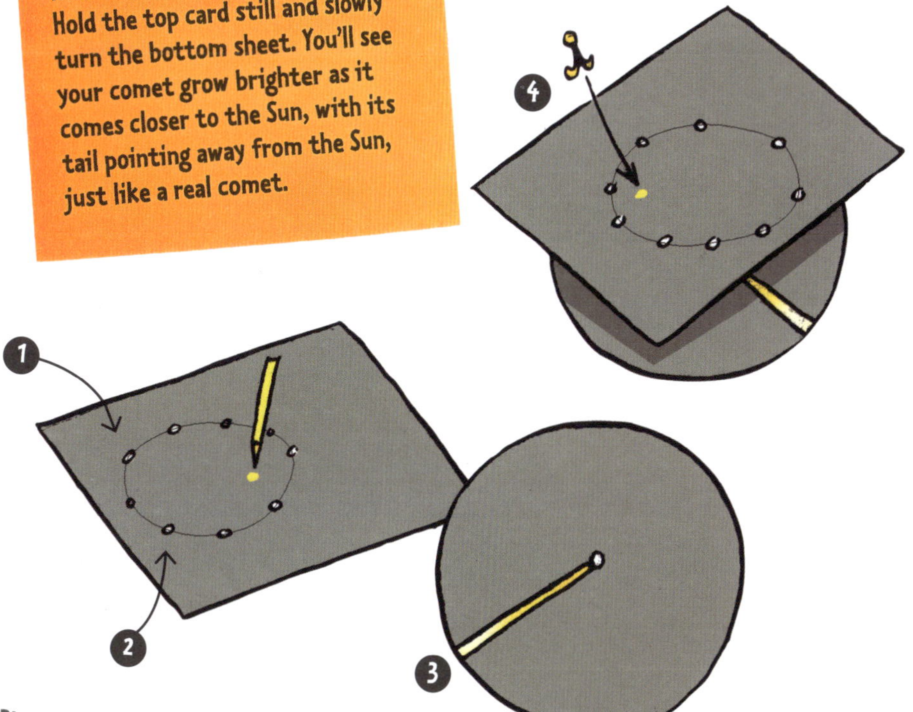

Exploring space

Since the first spacecraft was launched in 1957, astronauts have landed on the Moon, robot spacecraft have explored the Solar System and telescopes have probed distant parts of the Universe. You might be able to explore space yourself in the future!

Space missions

1957 first spacecraft, Sputnik 1.

1961 first person in space, Yuri Gagarin in Vostok 1.

1969 first manned Moon landing, Apollo 11.

1998 the first part of the International Space Station is launched.

2012 the Curiosity rover lands on Mars.

ROBOT EXPLORERS

The furthest that people have travelled from Earth is the Moon, but robot spacecraft have now flown past, orbited or landed on every planet in the Solar System. Some spacecraft have used their instruments to look far out into the rest of the Universe.

▼ The New Horizons space probe is on its way to the dwarf planet Pluto.

The biggest **spacecraft** ever built is the International Space Station. It's **so big** that it can be seen without a telescope. It looks like **a star**.

MARS ROVER

The Curiosity rover moves around Mars studying the surface and atmosphere. Its robot arm can reach out to take a closer look at interesting rocks. Curiosity is the fourth rover to be sent to Mars since 1996, and it's the biggest. Scientists decide where it should go and then send it instructions by radio.

▼ Curiosity is a mobile science laboratory the size of a car that landed on Mars in 2012 to study the red planet.

Balloon rocket

The rockets that launch spacecraft power themselves into space on a jet of gas. Make a balloon rocket to see how this works.

SUPPLIES
string • drinking straw • long balloon • sticky tape

HOW TO MAKE

1. Tie one end of the string to something solid and secure, like a doorknob.

2. Thread the string through the drinking straw and tie the other end to something solid and secure several metres away, so that the string is tight.

3. Blow up the balloon and, while holding the neck, stick the balloon to the drinking straw with the sticky tape.

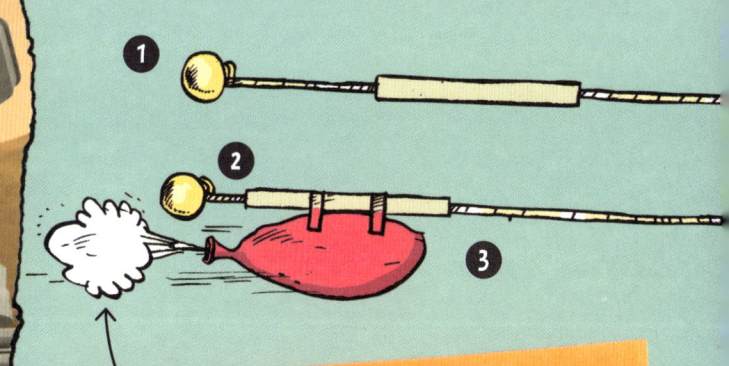

HOW TO USE
Let go of the balloon and watch it fly along the string. The air escaping from the balloon pushes it along, like the fiery jet of burning gas from a rocket. The pushing force that moves the balloon and a real rocket is called thrust.

SPACE TELESCOPES

Most telescopes are built on top of mountains, where they are above most of Earth's atmosphere. In the clear, thin air above the clouds, they get a better view of space. Some telescopes go one better — they have been launched into orbit around Earth.

▶ The Spitzer Space Telescope uses the heat given out by distant objects in space to make pictures of them. It took this picture of the Helix Nebula.

72

Earth

The living planet

Planet Earth is a tiny spinning rock in a vast universe, but we call it home. It is the only place we know about that can support life, because it has an atmosphere, water, land and just the right amount of light and heat from the Sun.

▼ The Sun is a vast ball of hydrogen gas, working like a nuclear reactor to make energy as light and heat.

COMFORT BLANKET

There is a thick blanket of invisible gases around the Earth (including oxygen, nitrogen and carbon dioxide). This is called the atmosphere. It keeps the planet warm and protects it from the Sun's radiation – a powerful, burning energy.

▼ As the Earth orbits around the Sun, seasons are created.

FOUR SEASONS

The Earth travels around the Sun once every 365 days, which gives us a year. Our planet is tilted, and the north and south halves take turns to lean towards the Sun for a time and get more heat and light. That time, or season, is called summer. It's colder and darker in places that tilt away from the Sun, so they experience winter.

MAGIC MOON

The Moon orbits Earth once about every 28 days because of a force called gravity. The Moon's gravity pulls on Earth's waters, causing them to rise and fall (tides).

▶ Waters in line with the Moon bulge — this is high tide (1). Low tides (2) are on the sides of Earth 90 degrees away from the Moon.

Big bang

Scientists believe the Universe began with a giant explosion called the Big Bang. Try this fun experiment to make a big bang of your own.

WARNING! Make sure you do this activity outside

SUPPLIES
kitchen roll • tablespoon • small cup • white vinegar small plastic bag that zips shut • bicarbonate of soda warm water

HOW TO MAKE
1. Put a tablespoon of bicarbonate of soda in the middle of a sheet of kitchen roll and twist the sheet to make a small packet.

2. Pour half a cup of vinegar into the plastic bag, and add a quarter of a cup of warm water.

3. Zip the bag shut leaving a gap just big enough for the bicarbonate of soda packet.

4. Carefully push the packet into the bag, but try to keep it out of the liquid while you zip the bag shut.

5. As you put the bag on the ground give it a bit of a shake and stand well back.

6. Wait and watch what happens!

LIFE ON EARTH

At first, Earth was far too hot for life. As it cooled, the atmosphere and oceans formed and life began to develop. Now there is a huge range of life, from tiny bacteria to millions of animals and plants.

WHAT, HOW, WHY?
You will use vinegar (an acid) to release carbon dioxide from bicarbonate of soda. The gas will be trapped in a bag, until the bag rips open under pressure and creates a mini-explosion.

Time line

13.7 BILLION YEARS AGO (BYA)
The Big Bang occurred, creating the Universe.

4.6 BYA
A cloud of gas and dust cooled to become our Sun and its planets — the Solar System.

4.5 BYA
A rocky planet the size of Mars crashed into Earth and created the Moon.

4–3.5 BYA
The first signs of life on Earth appeared.

2.4 BYA
Oxygen appeared in the atmosphere, which all plants and animals need.

Dynamic Earth

The land beneath your feet feels solid and still, but it is moving – very slowly! The Earth is covered in a rocky layer called the crust, with Earth's continents and oceans sitting on large pieces of this crust. These pieces, or plates, move because of liquid rock beneath them.

▼ Two plates meet in the middle of the Atlantic Ocean, at the Mid-Atlantic Ridge.

NORTH AMERICA
EUROPE
AFRICA
Mid-Atlantic Ridge
SOUTH AMERICA

MOVING PLATES
The large areas of rocky crust covering the Earth are broken up into giant pieces like a jigsaw puzzle. The moving plates cause continental drift – the way land moves over long periods of time.

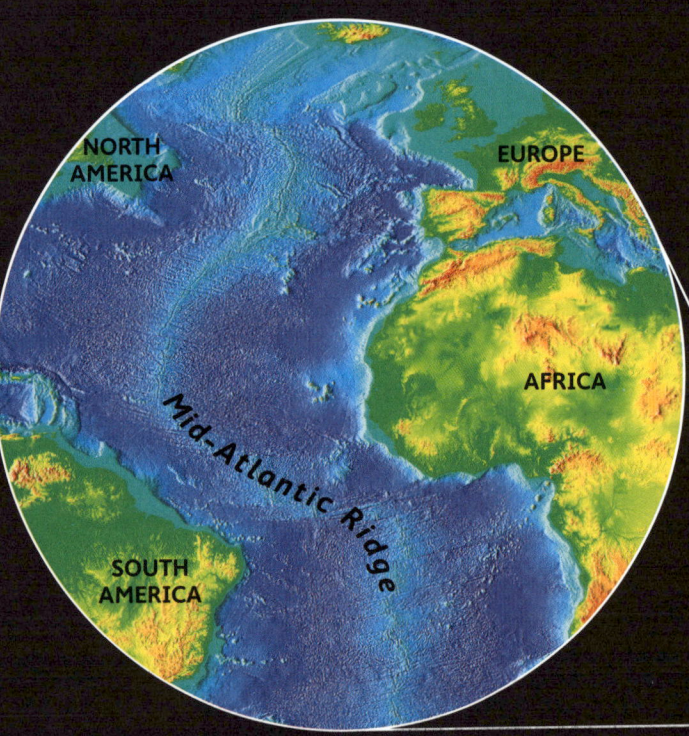

ATLANTIC OCEAN

GROW ZONE
When hot rock rises in the mantle it can force two plates apart. At the Mid-Atlantic Ridge new rock is added to the plate edges. This makes the ocean floor bigger and pushes the continents further apart.

▶ As rising rock forces the plates apart, a ridge is created. This is called a divergent boundary.

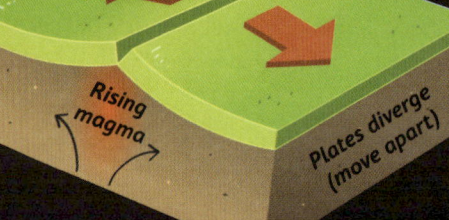

Rising magma
Plates diverge (move apart)

Chocolate planet

Discover how Earth's hot core makes the mantle move, creating convection currents and moving the crust.

WHAT, HOW, WHY?
The way that heat makes liquids, or air, move is called convection. Flows of heated liquid or air are called convection currents.

SUPPLIES
small saucepan (a glass one is best so you can see the convection currents from the side)
hot chocolate powder • milk

WHAT TO DO
1. Pour cold milk into a pan until it is about two-thirds full. The milk represents the mantle.

2. Shake the chocolate powder carefully over the surface to create the Earth's crust.

3. Ask a grown-up to help you gently heat the pan. If your pan has glass sides, you will see the 'mantle' moving with convection currents. Then you will see it begin to bubble up and break through the 'crust'.

After you have finished the experiment you can stir the chocolate powder into the milk to create a delicious hot drink!

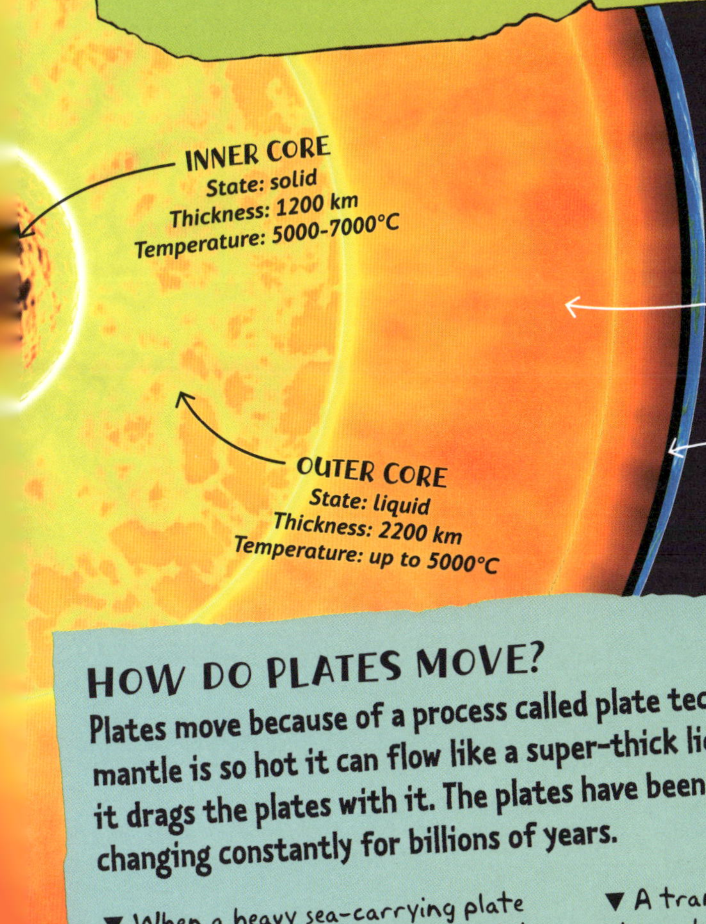

INNER CORE
State: solid
Thickness: 1200 km
Temperature: 5000-7000°C

OUTER CORE
State: liquid
Thickness: 2200 km
Temperature: up to 5000°C

◀ If you could look inside the Earth you'd see three layers: core, mantle and crust.

MANTLE
State: solid
Thickness: 3000 km
Temperature: up to 3500°C

CRUST
State: solid
Thickness: up to 50 km
Temperature: up to 1000°C

on the move

Today there are **seven major plates** and many smaller ones.

They move at a rate of up to **10 cm** a year.

As the crust moves away from a **divergent zone** it cools.

At the edge of the ocean, the **ocean crust** sinks under the edge of the continental crust and melts.

Scientists are still trying to work out exactly how and why **plates move**.

HOW DO PLATES MOVE?

Plates move because of a process called plate tectonics. The Earth's mantle is so hot it can flow like a super-thick liquid, and as it flows it drags the plates with it. The plates have been shifting and changing constantly for billions of years.

▼ When a heavy sea-carrying plate pushes against a land-carrying plate, the heavier plate sinks below the other at a subduction zone.

▼ A transform fault is a place where two plates slide past one another.

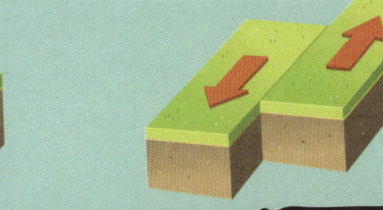

Explosive eruptions

When a volcano erupts, there may be rivers of scorching liquid rock, clouds of toxic ash or even giant rock-bombs raining down from the skies. This is one of the planet's most incredible, natural and deadly events – and a sign that Earth's fiery interior is on the move.

INSIDE A VOLCANO
As layers of lava (1) erupt they build up into layers (2) that create a cone-shaped volcano. A chamber beneath the volcano holds a pool of magma (3) and the channels through which the magma flows are called vents (4).

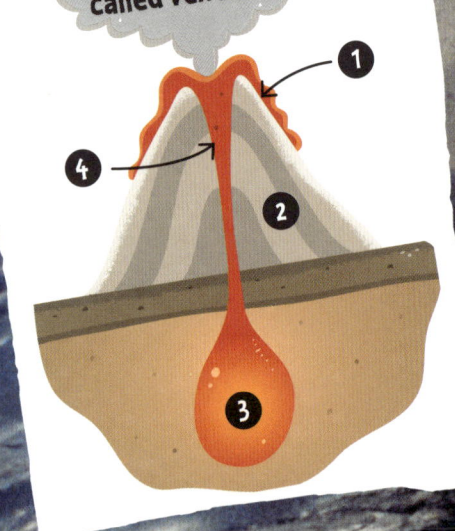

HOT ROCK
Melted rock in the Earth's mantle is called magma. Where the crust is thin and pressure builds up, magma can break through and pour out, erupting as lava.

VOLCANIC STATES
Active = erupting
Dormant = between eruptions
Extinct = not expected to erupt again

Famous volcanoes

AD 79 Mount Vesuvius
Rock, ash and toxic gas destroyed the Roman towns of Pompeii and Herculaneum.

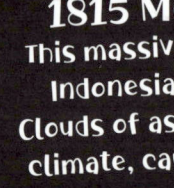

1815 Mount Tambora
This massive volcano exploded in Indonesia, causing tsunamis. Clouds of ash changed the world's climate, causing famine and war.

INSTANT IMPACT
A volcanic eruption can immediately affect the lives of people nearby, but its effects may be felt much further away. Clouds of dust and ash may spread all over the world, blocking out sunlight and changing the weather for years afterwards.

◀ Fountains and rivers of red-hot lava erupt from a shield volcano in Hawaii.

Make a mud-flow
After flash floods, mudflows are common on mountains and volcanoes. The way the mud moves is strange because, combined with water, it can flow freely, or become suddenly very gloopy. It's called a non-Newtonian fluid and you can make your own version. Prepare to be amazed!

SUPPLIES
water • cup • wooden spoon
cornflour • deep bowl or container

WHAT TO DO
Pour a cup of cornflour into the container. Add half a cup of water and mix it up.

Experiment with the mixture by:
- grabbing a handful of the mixture and squeezing it
- sticking the end of the wooden spoon in it
- stirring it slowly then quickly

Can you work out what actions make it liquid-like, and what makes it suddenly go solid?

TYPES AND SHAPES
Mountain-shaped volcanoes are called cone volcanoes, and they are found on land and under the sea. Other types are broader and flatter, so they are called shield volcanoes.

▶ This volcano on the island of Luzon in the Philippines is one of the most perfect examples of a cone volcano.

1883 Krakatoa
The volcanic island of Krakatoa was almost blown apart by a massive eruption, causing a huge loss of life.

1902 Mount Pelée
An eruption on the island of Martinique wiped out the city of St Pierre with searing winds at more than 1000°C.

1991 Mount Pinatubo
Millions of tons of magma and toxic gases polluted the atmosphere, reducing the world's temperature for several years.

Rattle and roll

Huge amounts of energy are released when plates move suddenly. Solid rock trembles and shudders, causing tiny tremors to enormous earthquakes, which can sometimes have dreadful effects.

▶ A sudden movement where the Eurasian and Indian plates meet caused a huge earthquake to hit Nepal in 2015. About 9000 people died and 3.5 million lost their homes.

EARTHQUAKES
Most earthquakes occur at the edges of tectonic plates. As the plates move they may get stuck, until a sudden release of pressure allows a big movement that causes tremors, or shakes.

How big?
The size of an earthquake is recorded using equipment called a seismometer, and measured using the Moment Magnitude Scale. It starts at 1 and can go up to 10 or above.

- ② you might notice some shaking
- ④ objects fall off shelves, little damage
- ⑥ shaking felt far away, damage to buildings
- ⑧ major damage, buildings collapse
- ⑩ total or near-total destruction

FOCUS!

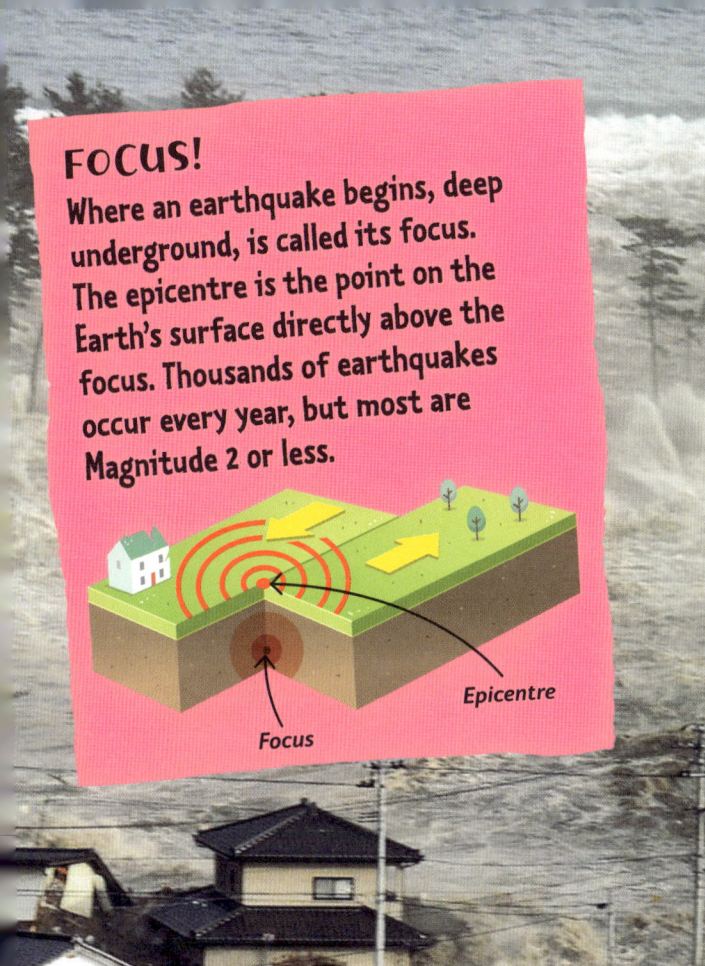

Where an earthquake begins, deep underground, is called its focus. The epicentre is the point on the Earth's surface directly above the focus. Thousands of earthquakes occur every year, but most are Magnitude 2 or less.

Focus
Epicentre

◀ A tsunami can sweep over land with strength and speed, destroying everything in its way.

NATURAL DISASTER

In 2004 one of the world's biggest recorded earthquakes occurred in the Indian Ocean. The giant tsunami hit land in 15 countries, with waves that reached 20 m in height. It became one of the worst natural disasters ever witnessed.

Make a seismometer

Follow these steps to make a simple seismometer and measure movement.

What happens to the line when you tap the box with more force?

SUPPLIES
cardboard box • scissors • plastic cup • marker pen • sticky tack • string • small stones • paper

HOW TO MAKE

1. Cut the flaps off the box and lie it on its side. Carefully make two small holes in the top.

2. Lay a piece of paper in the bottom of the box.

3. Cut a small hole in the base of the cup for the pen to fit into, and two holes on opposite sides of the rim.

4. Secure the pen (point side out) with sticky tack.

5. Half fill the cup with stones to weigh it down.

6. Run string through the other two holes in the cup, and through the holes in the box, so the cup hangs down.

7. Hold the string so the pen touches the paper and, once it's in the right position, tie the string.

8. Now try tapping the box gently, while pulling the paper towards you. The pen creates a recording of the movement.

81

Water world

Seen from space, Earth is a blue planet with swirling white clouds, thanks to the huge amount of water it holds. It is because of this water that there is life, and most living things exist in the oceans.

▼ Coral reefs grow in shallow water. They need sunlight and water that is warm and clean.

ON THE MOVE
Water in the ocean is always on the move. Wind and warmth together whip up the surface water, creating waves. The oceans have currents flowing in huge circles called gyres. Cool water flows closer to the seabed.

▶ A skilled surfer can balance on the crest of a wave. It's a thrilling ride to shore!

OCEAN POTION
Ocean water contains many dissolved gases and salts, as well as tiny animals and plants. It's home to more life than any other habitat on Earth, from blue whales – the largest animals to ever live – to the thumb-sized krill they eat.

EXTREME OCEAN
Surfers make the most of giant waves, but oceans can be dangerous. When two waves crash into each other they can create a rogue wave, which at more than 10 m tall, can sink a ship. Unusually high tides may flood towns and villages.

Disappearing act

Salt dissolves in water, which means you can't see it, but it is still there. Prove this for yourself with a simple experiment.

SUPPLIES
glass measuring jug • dessert spoon • hot water
table salt • clean baking tray with edges

WHAT TO DO
1. Pour two heaped dessert spoons of salt into 250 ml of hot water in the measuring jug.

2. Notice how the water turns cloudy, but soon begins to turn clear.

3. Stir the mixture until it turns completely clear.

4. You've now made a solution of salt and water (it's called a solution because the salt has dissolved).

5. Carefully pour the solution into the clean baking tray and leave it to dry, perhaps outside in the sun or near a radiator. For a faster result you can put the baking tray in the oven, on a low heat, until the water has all gone.

WHAT, HOW, WHY?
As the solution warms up the water evaporates (turns from a liquid to water vapour, which is a gas). There is no water to keep the salt dissolved, so it returns to being solid crystals of salt.

DIVING DEEP
Submersibles are used to explore the deep ocean. They have revealed a mysterious world of bizarre creatures that can survive in an extreme environment at a depth of 5000 m, where the water is cold and no light can reach.

▶ Deep-sea vessels such as Mir-1, are strong to withstand the force of tonnes of water pushing from all sides.

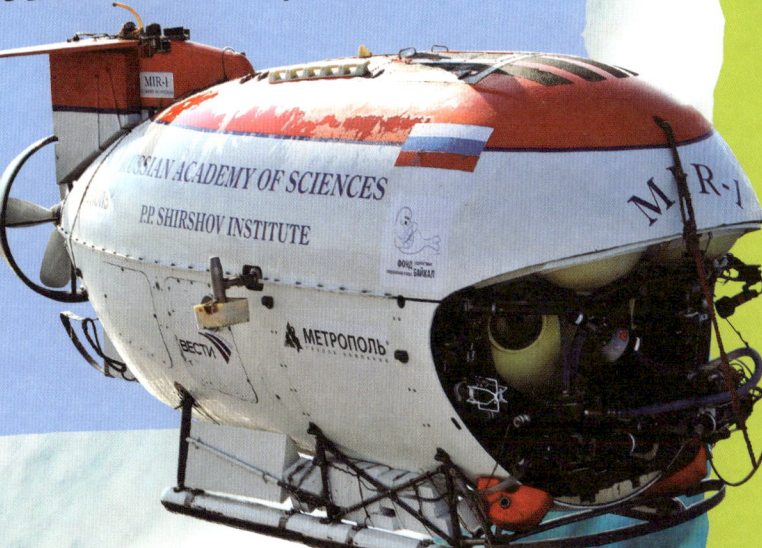

The five oceans

PACIFIC OCEAN
The largest ocean, covering more than 160 million square kilometres, with twice as much water as the next largest ocean, the Atlantic.

ATLANTIC OCEAN
A giant spreading rift runs down the middle and marks where the Atlantic is growing.

INDIAN OCEAN
The warmest of the three biggest oceans.

ARCTIC OCEAN
The smallest ocean is around the North Pole and partly covered in ice all year.

SOUTHERN OCEAN
Surrounds the continent of Antarctica.

Early life

No one knows what turned Earth from a hot, steamy space rock into a lush, green planet of life. All we do know is that 3.5 billion years ago tiny bacteria – a simple form of life – already existed. They appeared at about the same time the oceans formed.

ALL CHANGE
Since those early days in Earth's history, life has flourished and there are now billions of living things, and many millions of species – most of them are still waiting to be discovered.

525 million years ago:
Explosion of life in the oceans

VARIETY OF LIFE
As scientists uncover the secrets of the past they have revealed the long, and complex, story of life on Earth. As the planet changes, so do the animals and plants that inhabit it – and this has created a huge variety of life forms.

4–3.5 billion years ago:
Bacteria appear

▲ This diagram shows the evolution of life, from the very first organisms that appeared more than 3000 billion years ago to modern humans.

84

150–190 million years ago: First flowering plants

230–210 million years ago: First dinosaurs and mammals appear

150 million years ago: First birds appear

Evolution through time

1 Simple cells
2 Cyanobacteria
3 Cnidarians (soft-bodied animals)
4 *Dickinsonia* (early marine animal)
5 *Anomalocaris* (arthropod – animals with segmented bodies and no backbone)
6 Cockroach (insect)
7 Cycad (cone-bearing plant)
8 Coelacanth (fish)
9 *Diadectes* (reptile-like amphibian)
10 *Dimetrodon* (mammal-like reptile)
11 Plesiosaur (marine reptile)
12 *Liliensternus* (dinosaur)
13 Pterosaur (flying reptile)
14 Brachiosaur (large dinosaur)
15 Magnolia (flowering plant)
16 *Archaeopteryx* (early bird)
17 *Quetzalcoatlus* (pterosaur – flying reptile)
18 *Tyrannosaurus rex* (dinosaur)
19 Moa (flightless bird)
20 *Plesiadapis* (mammal)
21 *Paracetherium* (rhinoceros-like mammal)
22 *Smilodon* (carnivorous mammal)
23 *Macrauchenia* (hoofed mammal)
24 Wolf (carnivorous mammal)
25 *Homo sapiens* (modern human)

EVOLUTION

The way that living things adapt and change over time is called evolution. Living things that do not evolve eventually die out – this is extinction.

▶ The last dodo was seen in 1662. Humans caused its extinction.

85

What is a biome?

A biome is a population of animals and plants in a particular type of environment. Every biome has a particular type of climate (set of weather patterns), soil and wetness.

▲ Herds of African elephants live on the savannah.

▲ A polar bear's habitat includes land, ice and seawater.

GRASSLAND
Grasslands have less water all year round than forests, but are wetter than deserts. In Africa, grassland is called savannah, but in other parts of the world grassland is known as prairie, pampas or steppe.

POLAR
The winter is long and cold in a polar biome and the land is covered in ice for most, or all, of the year.

Amazing adaptations

A fennec fox's big ears help it to lose excess heat in the Sahara Desert.

Polar bear fur is made up of hollow hairs. They trap heat near an animal's skin, helping to keep it warm.

A giraffe's height allows it to feed on the upper leaves of trees in its grassland habitat. It wouldn't do so well in a polar biome!

▲ Amphibians, such as frogs and salamanders, need wet habitats.

◀ Koalas live in dry forests of gum trees.

TEMPERATE

Temperate places rarely experience extreme weather and there are four seasons. Woodland and conifer forests are examples of temperate biomes.

Turn the page to discover more biomes

DESERT

Rain rarely falls in a desert, making this one of the most challenging environments for plant and animal life.

▲ Desert snakes can survive a long time without food or water.

▲ The Arabian oryx is adapted for life in the desert. However, it has been hunted and is now rare.

87

Precious places

Each biome is unique, relying on a delicate balance of conditions. A biome contains multiple habitats – the word we use to describe where an animal species lives.

◄ The pattern and colour of this snow leopard's fur helps it hide in its habitat.

MOUNTAIN

The habitats at the foot of the mountain are very different to those at the top, where it is often cold and dry. Few trees can grow high on a mountain.

▲ Leafcutter ants build giant nests underground.

◄ A huge beak helps this toucan reach the juiciest fruit at the tip of the branches.

TROPICAL FOREST

Rainy days and strong sunshine all year make tropical forests a supe[r] habitat for millions o[f] plants and animals.

▼ Crocodiles are superb swimmers, but they can run fast too.

▲ Thick, soft feathers keep a snowy owl warm.

TUNDRA

Cold, bleak and treeless plains between the Arctic and temperate forests form the tundra biome. Below the soil, the ground is permanently frozen.

FRESHWATER

Rivers, lakes and ponds are home to fish and many invertebrates. Other animals come to the water to drink, or catch prey.

◀ Coral reefs make a perfect habitat for many ocean animals.

OCEAN

The largest, most mysterious of all Earth's biomes, the oceans contain the smallest and largest animals on the planet.

89

The water cycle

The amount of water on the planet and in its atmosphere stays the same, but it is always on the move between the land, the oceans and the air. The way that water moves around the Earth is called the water cycle.

WATERY PLANET
Water exists on Earth in three different states, depending on its temperature: solid (ice), liquid (water) and gas (water vapour).

Sunlight warms the oceans and water evaporates. It rises into the sky

Make a mini water cycle

Create a mini water cycle to watch how water can turn from a liquid to a gas and back again.

SUPPLIES
large plastic bowl • small mug • cling film
cold water • jug

WHAT TO DO

1. Place a clean, dry mug in the middle of the bowl. Make sure the edges of the bowl are taller than the mug.

2. Carefully pour cold water into the bowl (but not inside the mug) until it is about 2/3 full of water. The water represents the ocean and the mug is like a mountain on land.

3. Cover the bowl with cling film. Make sure it is tightly sealed around the edge of the bowl.

4. Leave the bowl somewhere warm (in the sun or by a radiator). The time you will need to leave the bowl depends on the temperature.

WHAT, HOW, WHY?
The heat gives the water the energy it needs to turn into an invisible vapour – it evaporates. The vapour cools when it touches the cling film and turns back into a liquid – it condenses. Water droplets appear on the underside of the cling film and start to drip back into the 'ocean' and some water will drip into the mug, like rain falling on mountains.

Raging water

The Colorado River has eroded through 1.8 km of rock to create the **Grand Canyon**.

The tallest waterfall in the world is the **Angel Falls** in Venezuela, where water plummets nearly 1 km from a mountaintop!

The mighty Zambezi River tumbles over **Victoria Falls**, which is also known as 'the smoke that thunders'.

The Niagara Falls in North America is the **largest** waterfall by volume of water. Erosion is causing it to move back by about 30 cm every year.

Droplets of water in the clouds get bigger and heavier until they turn to rain or snow over mountains

Water vapour creates clouds and wind moves the clouds towards land

Rain, or snow, falls

As rivers flow from high areas they move fast and with high energy, eroding the rocks to create valleys

Frozen rivers of ice occur in regions near the North and South Pole. They are called glaciers

Rivers with low energy wind across flatter land, creating meanders

After heavy rain, some water forms floods, flowing over the ground into the rivers or sea. This is called run-off

Water collects in rivers and flows towards the sea

At a river mouth, debris is dropped creating huge fan-shaped areas called deltas

SUBTERRANEAN SPECTACLE

Some water seeps or flows through the rock. This groundwater can carve out huge caverns and tunnels.

▶ Underground, minerals in groundwater can create enormous stony formations called stalactites and stalagmites.

Air and atmosphere

As the Sun warms the planet it heats the atmosphere and causes convection currents. They make the air move (creating wind) and carry moisture and heat all around the planet, giving us a world of wonderful weather – from snowstorms to sunny days.

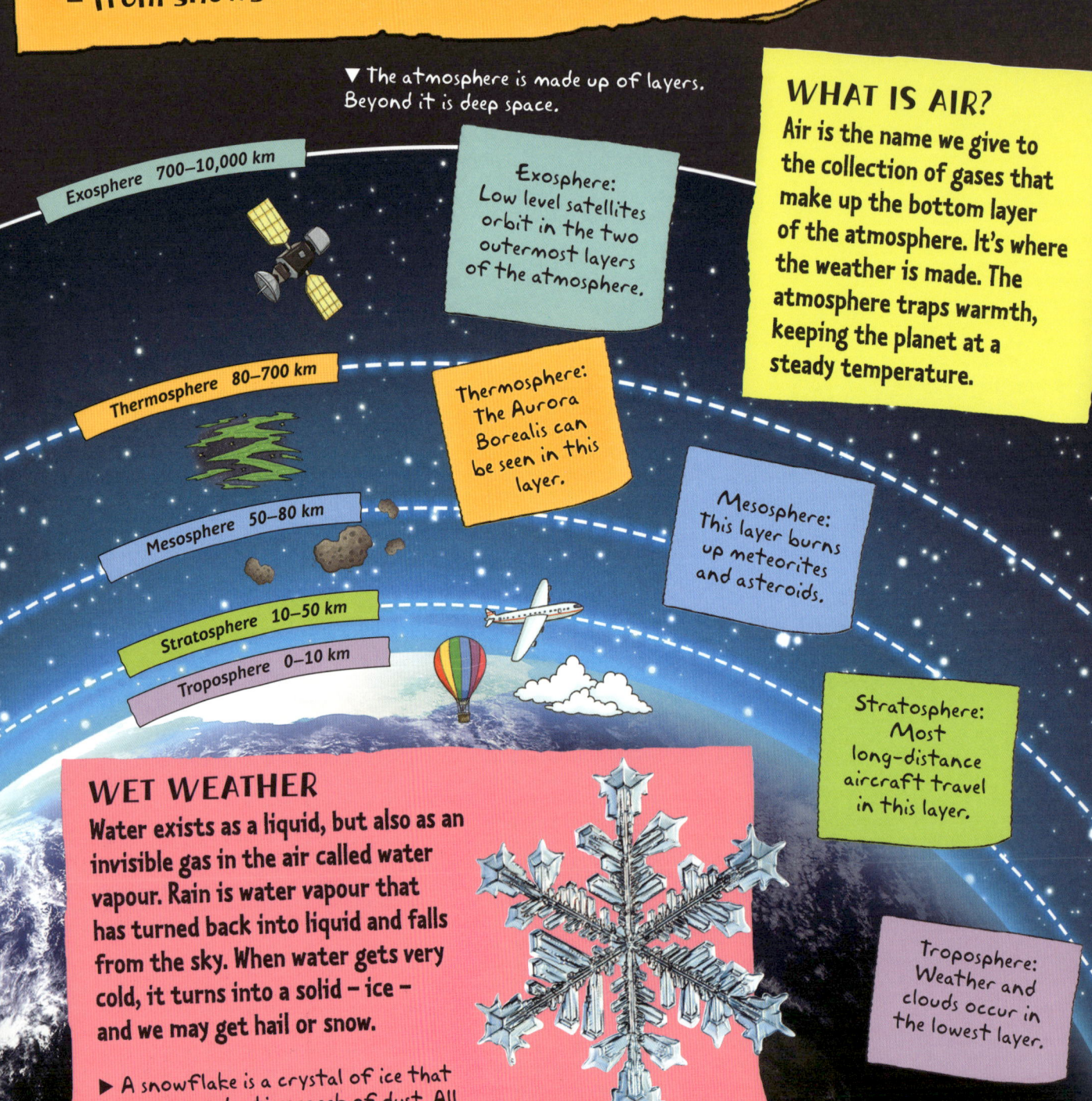

▼ The atmosphere is made up of layers. Beyond it is deep space.

Exosphere 700–10,000 km

Exosphere: Low level satellites orbit in the two outermost layers of the atmosphere.

Thermosphere 80–700 km

Thermosphere: The Aurora Borealis can be seen in this layer.

Mesosphere 50–80 km

Mesosphere: This layer burns up meteorites and asteroids.

Stratosphere 10–50 km

Troposphere 0–10 km

Stratosphere: Most long-distance aircraft travel in this layer.

Troposphere: Weather and clouds occur in the lowest layer.

WHAT IS AIR?
Air is the name we give to the collection of gases that make up the bottom layer of the atmosphere. It's where the weather is made. The atmosphere traps warmth, keeping the planet at a steady temperature.

WET WEATHER
Water exists as a liquid, but also as an invisible gas in the air called water vapour. Rain is water vapour that has turned back into liquid and falls from the sky. When water gets very cold, it turns into a solid – ice – and we may get hail or snow.

▶ A snowflake is a crystal of ice that forms around a tiny speck of dust. All have six sides, but no two are identical.

ELECTRIC SKY
When water or ice crystals in a cloud bump into each other they make static electricity. If there is enough of it the cloud charges up like a battery, causing a flash of lightning to zip through the sky. The heat and energy from the lightning makes the air expand around it, producing a clap of thunder!

▼ Bolts of electricity fork through the dark sky.

Lightning strikes

A single flash of lightning can release enough energy to power a light bulb for six months. The spark you'll create here is much smaller! Try this experiment on a cool, dry day and turn off the lights to see the flash.

SUPPLIES
tin foil • plastic fork • rubber glove • blown up balloon (biodegradable) wooden chopping board

WHAT TO DO
1. Fold tin foil around the head of a plastic fork, keeping it flat and smooth.

2. Wearing the rubber glove to hold the balloon, rub the balloon over your hair for one minute.

3. Place the balloon on the wooden board.

4. Using your gloved hand, touch the fork to the balloon, so the tin foil is in contact with the surface, and hold it there.

5. Using your bare hand, touch the foil and watch for the flash!

WHAT, HOW, WHY?
Rubbing the balloon on your hair generates static electricity, freeing lots of tiny particles called electrons. They move towards the tin foil, but can't escape until you touch it with your bare finger. The electrons zap across to your skin and down to the ground, creating a flash of electricity.

Types of cloud

CIRRUS
Where: high in the sky
Appear: wispy like tufts of hair
Made of: ice crystals
Weather: a change of weather is on the way

ALTOCUMULUS
Where: medium level
Appear: white or grey clumps
Made of: water droplets and ice crystals
Weather: settled and dry

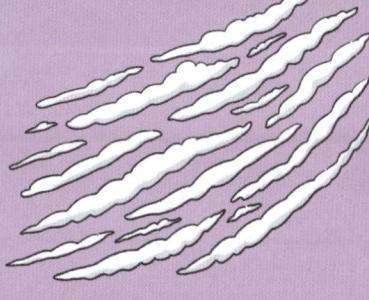

CUMULONIMBUS
Where: from low sky to high in the sky
Appear: large, tall cloud
Made of: ice crystals and water vapour
Weather: rain, possibly thunderstorms

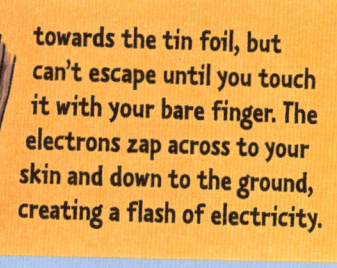

93

Extreme weather

Scientists may predict the weather, but there is nothing they can do to control the ever-changing mixture of gases, water and solar energy that create the weather. Sometimes extreme weather hits the planet with extraordinary, devastating effects.

▼ Snowstorms occur during winter in temperate and polar places.

WHITE OUT
When heavy snow and strong winds work together they can create terrible blizzards, or snowstorms. In the worst cases, thick blankets of snow cover the ground and dense, falling snow makes it impossible to see your hand in front of your face.

Tornado in a bottle
Explore the way that liquids spin. Spinning air works the same way to create tornadoes.

SUPPLIES
water • jug • clear plastic bottle with lid
washing up liquid

HOW TO MAKE
1. Using a jug, fill the plastic bottle with water until it's half full.
2. Add a few drops of washing up liquid.
3. Screw on the lid of the bottle, making sure it's on tightly.
4. Turn the bottle upside down and hold it by the neck. Spin the bottle in a circular motion so the water swirls around inside.
5. Stop and watch your mini tornado forming in the water!

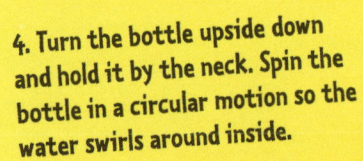

WHAT, HOW, WHY?
The whirling funnel shape you can see is called a vortex. When moving air (wind) gets energy from the Sun and warms up, it can also make a vortex.

94

SAND STORM

When hot winds scoop up dry sand in the Sahara they can create violent dust storms, called haboobs. As the giant clouds of sand sweep across the land, they engulf buildings in a dense red 'mist'.

▼ A sandstorm can occur after a time of drought (when there has been no rain).

SPINNING TWISTERS

A twister, or tornado, is a powerful column of air that spins at great speed, causing damage or destruction to anything in its path. Most tornadoes form over land, from a thunderstorm.

▼ A whirling tornado connects a cloud above to the ground below.

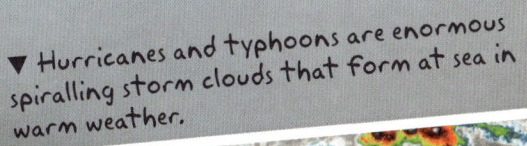

▼ Hurricanes and typhoons are enormous spiralling storm clouds that form at sea in warm weather.

Record breakers

HOTTEST TEMPERATURE
56.7°C
Death Valley, USA,
June 1913

COLDEST TEMPERATURE
−89.2°C
Vostok Station,
Antarctica, July 1983

MOST RAINY DAYS IN A YEAR
350
Mount Wai'ale'ale,
Hawaii

HEAVIEST HAILSTONES
1 kg
Bangladesh, India,
April 1986

DEEPEST SNOW
12 m
Honshu Island,
Japan, 1927

DRIEST PLACE
Less than 0.75 mm
of rain a year
Atacama Desert, Chile

Weather science

People have always tried to understand the weather. They have kept a close eye on the sky and tried to work out what a red sky or a misty moon might mean. Today we can rely on weather science, or meteorology. We can measure and record details from around the world.

How do we measure it?

As well as thermometers and rain gauges, a basic **weather station** will also include these instruments:

Barometers forecast weather conditions as air pressure rises or falls, recording it in units called millibars (mb). Electronic pressure sensors are now included in many phones.

Anemometers measure wind speed. You may have spotted them on top of some buildings or bridges – they look like whirling cups or vanes.

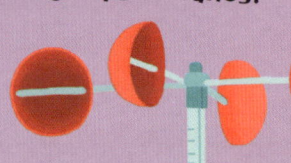

WEATHER ELECTRONICS

Modern weather science depends on machines that collect data automatically. These might be in weather satellites in space, on ships and buoys in the ocean, fitted to aircraft, or attached to balloons that go into the upper atmosphere. The data is fed back to computers.

▶ Meteorologists studying the effects of severe thunderstorms prepare to launch a weather balloon.

AND NOW, THE WEATHER...

Satellite data from computers is used to put together the day's weather forecasts on television and the Internet. Forecasts are now more accurate than ever before.

◀ Weather apps on smart phones let you personalize forecasts, wherever you are in the world.

96

Build a barometer

Barometers don't need to be high-tech. This one uses a balloon and a needle to record changes in air pressure.

SUPPLIES
scissors • biodegradable balloon • glass jar • rubber band • sticky tape • plastic sewing needle • reusable drinking straw • PVA glue • A4 light card • felt-tip pen

HOW TO MAKE
1. Use the scissors to cut off the 'neck' of the balloon. Stretch the rest over the top of the jar and secure it tightly with the rubber band.

2. Tape the needle to the end of the straw.

3. Use the glue to stick the needle-free end of the straw on top of the jar.

4. Mark the card with HIGH and LOW as shown, and place it beside the jar. Mark a line at the level of the needle.

Ask an adult for help!

HOW IT WORKS
Air is trapped inside the jar. When the air pressure outside the jar is higher than the pressure inside, it presses down on the balloon and pushes the needle upwards. When the pressure outside the jar drops, the air inside the jar pushes the balloon upwards, making the needle drop.

HOW TO USE
Mark off the changes to the needle's position every hour or two. Did the air pressure go up or down over the course of a day?

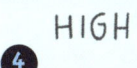

FINDING OUT THE FACTS

Data gathered from one source, such as the soil moisture and salinity (saltiness) satellite known as SMOS, can be combined with information from many other satellites, aircraft, ships and weather stations. This helps us to understand the big picture of climate and how it is changing.

▼ This European Space Agency satellite orbits the Earth, measuring soil moisture and the saltiness of the oceans. It helps us understand climate and the water cycle.

97

Earth's resources

Iron, oil, gold, wood and gas – these are just some of the world's resources that we use every day. Earth provides us with the materials we need to work, learn, build and power our homes, and feed ourselves.

How is it made?

Natural materials come from animals, plants or from the ground, like:

Wood
Leather
Oil
Cotton
Gold

Silk
Wool
Iron
Sand

Synthetic materials are man-made, often in factories. Paper is made from wood; plastic is made from oil; glass is made from sand; nylon is made from oil, and steel is made from iron and carbon.

MIGHTY METALS
Metals are very useful materials because they conduct heat and electricity. They are strong but can be moulded into different shapes.

▼ At a quarry, stone, slate, gravel and other resources are removed from the ground.

WHERE DOES RUBBER COME FROM?
It comes from rubber trees! Latex is taken from a tree and turned into rubber – a natural material that is soft and stretchy. It's used in tyres because of these properties, and because it helps a wheel grip on to a road surface.

Rock cakes

Rock cakes, like real rocks, are hard and lumpy. Thankfully they taste much better!

SUPPLIES
mixing bowl • weighing scales • wooden spoon
two forks • knife • baking tray • cooling rack

INGREDIENTS
350 g plain flour • ¼ teaspoon salt
2 teaspoons baking powder • 175 g light brown sugar
¼ teaspoon grated nutmeg • ¼ teaspoon mixed spice • 175 g butter • 125 g mixed fruit or sultanas • 1 large egg, lightly whisked
1–2 tablespoons milk

HOW TO MAKE
1. Heat the oven to gas mark 5 or 190°C (374°F).

2. Mix the flour, salt, baking powder, sugar, nutmeg and mixed spice in a bowl.

3. Chop up the butter into small slabs and use your fingertips to rub it into the mixture until it looks like breadcrumbs.

4. Stir in the fruit.

5. Add the whisked egg and mix together. Add milk if the mixture is dry.

6. Use two forks to make 10–12 spiky mounds of mixture evenly spaced on the baking tray.

7. Bake for 18–20 minutes and leave on a cooling rack before eating.

As you make the rock cakes, think about where all the things you are using come from, including the fuel that makes the oven hot. If you don't know the answer, use the internet to do some research.

USEFUL ROCKS
A rock is made of minerals, such as quartz, calcite and salt. Rocks can also contain metals, such as gold and iron, or precious gems like diamonds and emeralds.

FEEDING THE WORLD
Two million years ago our human ancestors hunted animals and found plants to eat. It was only about 11,500 years ago that early farmers learned how to keep animals and grow their own crops. Today, farming has a bigger impact on the Earth than ever before.

▲ Modern machinery has helped farmers to feed the world.

99

Powering the planet

Through human history, wood has been burned for heat and light. Today, we mostly rely on dirty fossil fuels to give us the energy we need to power a modern world. In the future, we will depend on cleaner, sustainable fuels — like solar, wind and water power.

WHAT ARE FOSSIL FUELS?

Oil, gas and coal are all types of fossil fuel, made millions of years ago from the remains of animals or plants. We take them from the ground, or under the sea, and burn them to generate electricity or fuel homes and vehicles.

▼ A solar panel uses sunlight to make electricity, while a leaf makes chemical energy from it.

▶ A group of wind turbines is called a wind farm.

WIND POWER

One wind turbine can generate enough electricity to power 1000 homes. They can be built on land or in the sea but they do need plenty of windy days to be useful.

PLANT POWER

Photovoltaic cells in a solar panel capture sunlight and turn it into power for light and heat, just as chloroplasts in a leaf capture the Sun's energy for a plant to use.

KEY
1. A leaf's transparent upper layer allows sunlight to pass into it.
2. The palisade layer contains chloroplasts, which capture light and turn it into fuel for the plant.

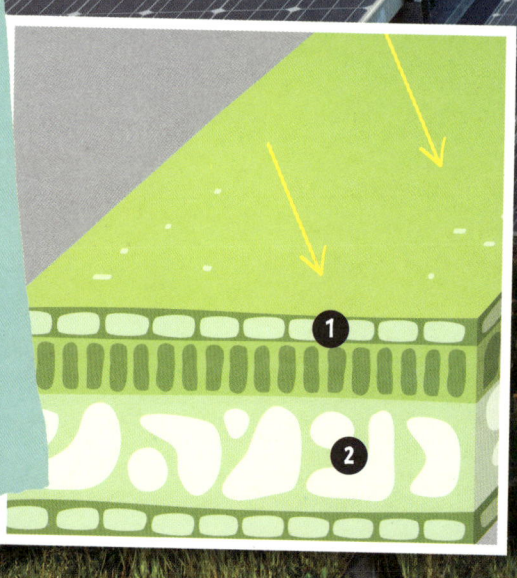

100

▼ Hot underground water can erupt in a cloud of steam. It is called a geyser.

HOT EARTH

The ground beneath our feet is warm, especially in places where there are hot springs or tectonic activity. That heat can be used as a source of energy. It's called geothermal energy.

Potato power!

Electric cars are becoming more popular because they use power stored in batteries instead of burning a fossil fuel. Make your own potato battery to power a clock.

SUPPLIES
2 big potatoes • 2 large galvanised nails
2 lengths of copper wire 3 cm long
3 alligator clips with leads • battery clock

WHAT TO DO
1. Remove the battery from the clock.

2. Label the potatoes '1' and '2'. This will help you attach the clips correctly later.

3. Push one galvanised nail halfway into an end of each potato.

4. Stick a piece of copper wire halfway into the other end of each potato. (The wire and the nail should not touch each other.)

5. Follow the diagram below to attach two alligator clips to the potatoes and the battery terminals in the clock.

6. Use the third alligator clip to join the two potatoes.

7. Your clock should start working again!

WHAT, HOW, WHY?
The potato conducts electricity between the two nails. The inside of a potato is acidic. The acid makes electrons leave the zinc nail and travel through the potato to the copper wire, creating an electric current, in just the same way that a battery does.

What is energy?

Energy is the **ability to do work**, or make things happen.

Energy can't be made or destroyed, but it can be **changed** from one type to another. Heat, light and electricity are three types of energy.

We get **light** and **heat** from the Sun's energy but we also get energy from fuels such as oil and gas.

Reduce, reuse, recycle

Protecting and caring for the Earth is an important job for everyone. There are simple steps we can all take to look after our big, beautiful planet and save its precious resources for the future.

Help the Earth picture

Create a picture to help remind people that keeping the world healthy and safe for all living things is a job for everyone.

SUPPLIES
plain paper • dinner plate • map of the world pencils • pens • paints • glue • scissors

HOW TO MAKE
1. On a plain piece of paper, draw around a large plate to create a circle – this is Earth.

2. Using the map, draw continents on the Earth and colour them in green. Colour the oceans blue.

3. On another piece of paper, draw around your hands and paint them any colour you like.

4. Cut out the Earth and hand shapes.

5. Glue the hands to the back of the Earth so they look as if they are holding the world.

6. On each 'finger' write your ideas for reducing pollution, such as 'Walk to school' or 'Turn off electric lights'.

FOCUS ON POLLUTION

Anything that contaminates (damages) the natural world is pollution. Oceans and coasts have become dirty places because rubbish, especially plastic, is thrown into rivers or seas. Marine pollution kills wildlife and damages habitats around the world.

▶ The V5 Seabin is like a floating bin for the sea. It can catch 3.9 kg of debris a day once it is installed in marinas, harbours and ports.

CLIMATE CHANGE

When fossil fuels are burned they release dangerous gases and chemicals into the air. These 'greenhouse gases' build up in the atmosphere and stop heat escaping into space. As the world gets warmer and weather patterns change, some animals and plants will struggle to survive.

▼ Plastiki's voyage was powered by wind, and solar panels.

THE FUTURE OF PLASTIC
Environmentalist David de Rothschild created his 18 m boat, Plastiki, from 12,500 plastic bottles and recycled waste. Plastiki sailed from California to Sydney in 2010 to raise awareness of the world's over-use of plastic.

◄ Around the world, people are giving up their time to clean beaches.

Reduce your eco-footprint by choosing to buy things that aren't wrapped up in lots of unnecessary packaging.

Recycling means turning waste into something we can use again. Glass, plastic, paper and aluminium can all be recycled.

Find other uses for things you don't need anymore, or give them away or sell them.

How long until it's gone?

Here's how long it takes for common rubbish to break down (decompose):

Plastic bag up to 500 years

Plastic bottle up to 450 years

Plastic straw up to 200 years

Drinks can up to 200 years

Crisp packets up to 80 years

Cigarette end up to 10 years

Apple core up to 2 months

103

Can climate change?

The weather is always changing, from one day to the next or with the passing seasons. Generally, these changes follow a regular pattern. But over thousands or millions of years a region's climate can change too, or even the climate of the planet as a whole.

What can we do?

These are some simple things you can do at home to help slow climate change:

1. Turn off electrical items when you're not using them.
2. Walk or cycle instead of using the car.
3. Reuse and recycle things instead of throwing them away.
4. Reduce food waste.
5. Put on a jumper when you feel a bit cold instead of turning on the heating.

TOO HOT

In the past, there have been cold ages, when ice stretched far beyond the polar regions. In between these ice ages, there have been warmer periods. At the moment, the planet should be slowly moving back towards one of these colder periods, but in fact Earth and its oceans are warming quickly – too quickly.

GAS OVERLOAD

Climate change may be affected by some natural processes. But nearly all scientists agree that humans play a big part in warming things up. We burn coal, oil or gas and push out fumes from our cars and factories into the atmosphere.

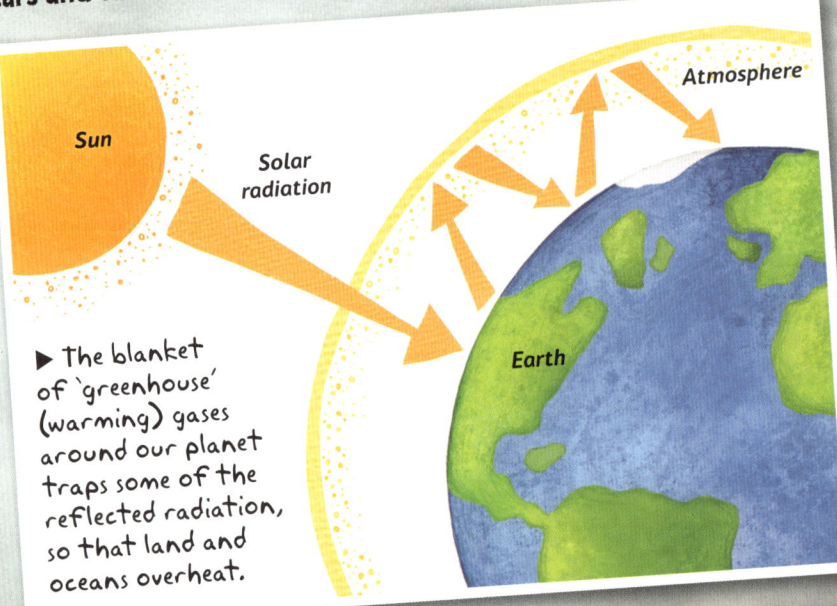

▶ The blanket of 'greenhouse' (warming) gases around our planet traps some of the reflected radiation, so that land and oceans overheat.

WHAT ABOUT THE FUTURE?
Global warming could upset weather patterns around the planet, with more violent storms, floods and drought, melting ice at the Poles and rising sea levels. To change course, we need to keep our planet clean and green, using renewable energy. Our survival may depend on it!

▼ Low-lying coral islands such as the Maldives in the Indian Ocean are at risk of disappearing if sea levels rise.

◀ The melting of Arctic ice can affect the ability of polar bears to hunt, rest and breed.

Be a weather historian

Find out if people think that the weather has changed over the years.

SUPPLIES
notebook • pen

WHAT TO DO
1. Interview grandparents or elderly neighbours. Do they think the weather is different from when they were young?

2. Can they remember any big storms, droughts or floods?

3. Have they noticed any changes to the growing season in gardens or parks? Are there new animals or insects to be seen?

4. Have there been big changes to factories and traffic in their lifetimes?

HOW TO USE
Write down their stories – there may be lessons to be learnt. If you interview more than one person, do their memories of big weather events match up?

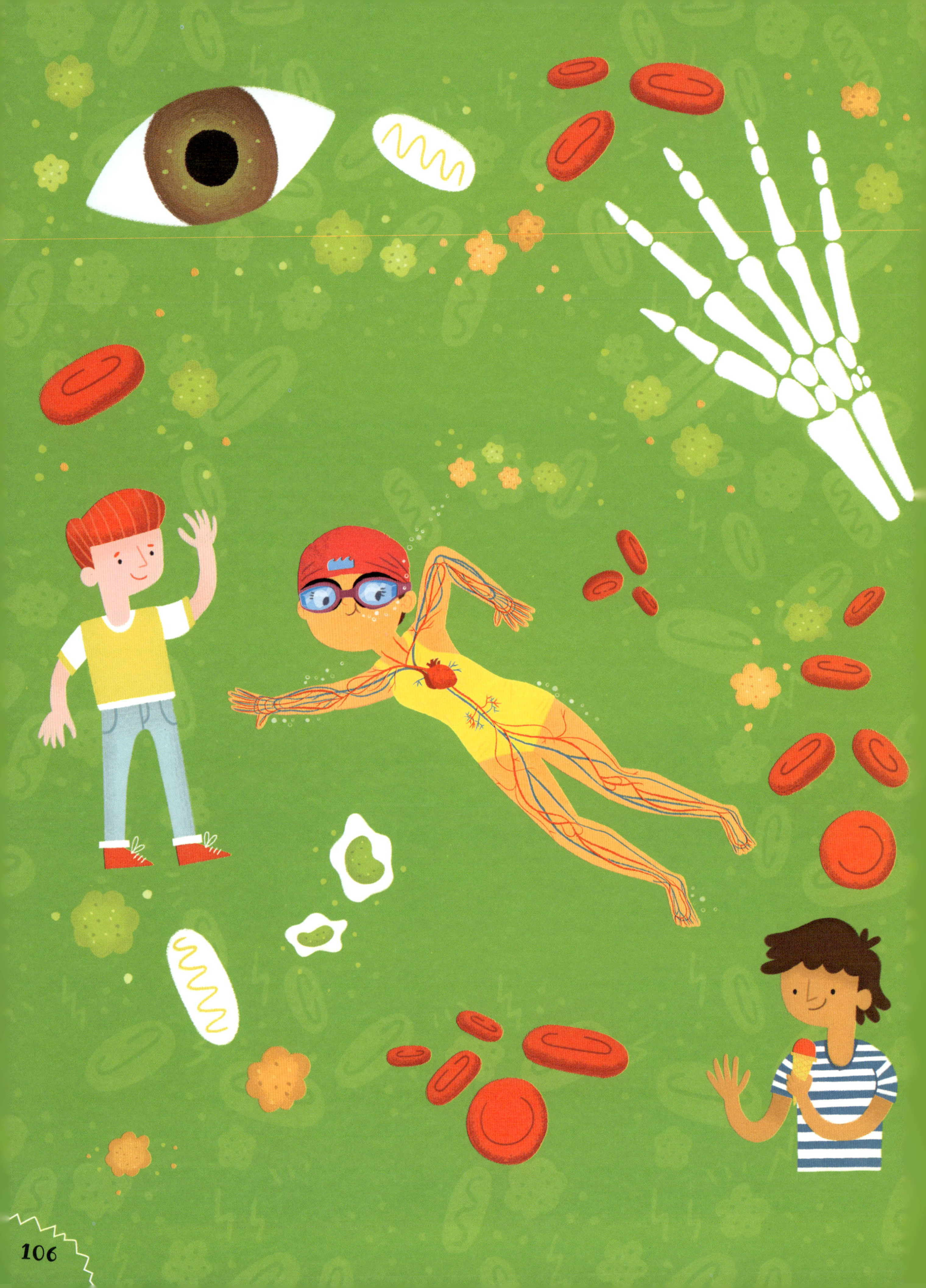

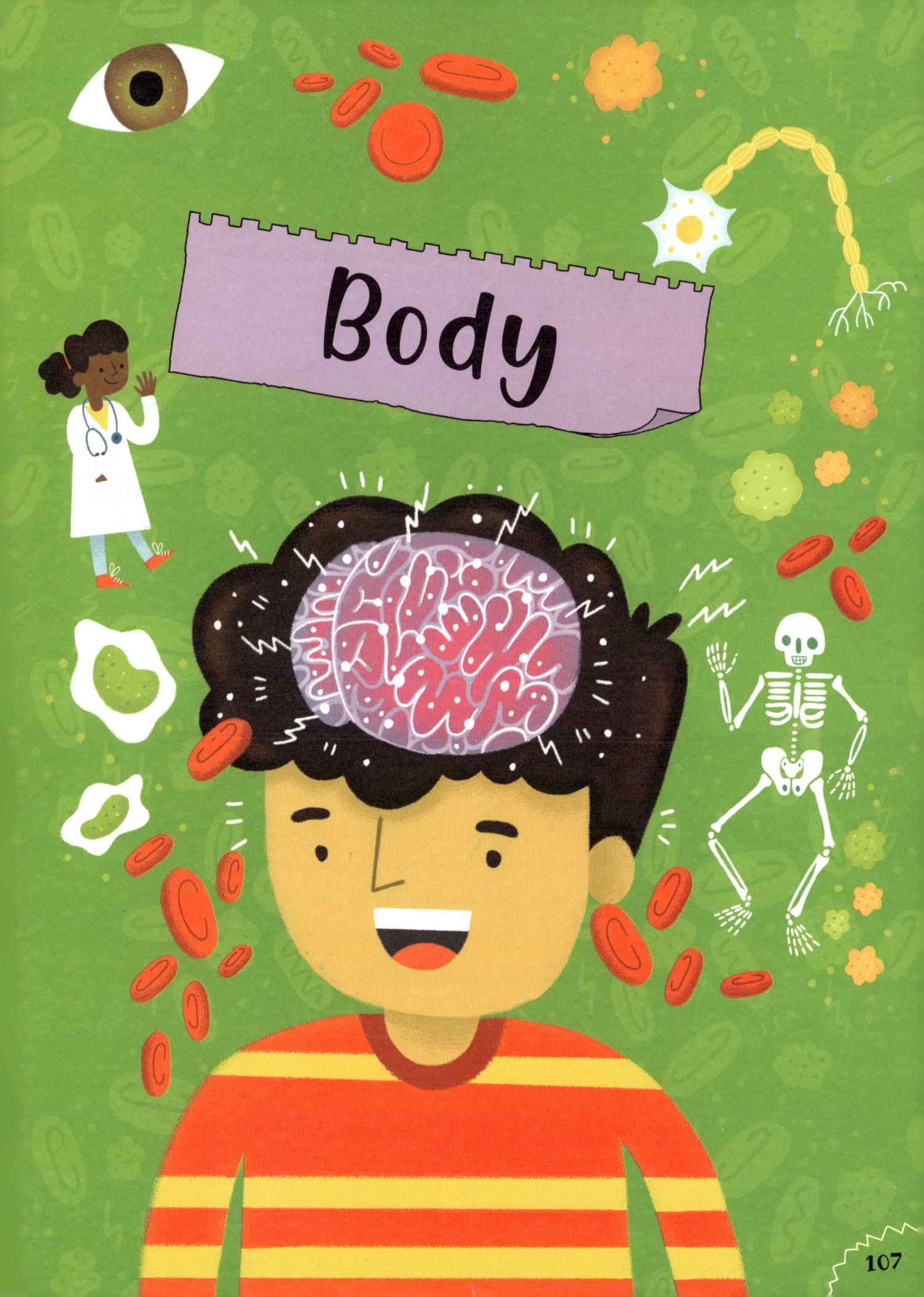

Body

Outside in

Together, your skin, hair and nails are known as the integumentary system. Skin is waterproof, and shields you from infection. It's also your body's largest sense organ, providing your brain with vital data about the world.

SUPER SURFACE

Your skin is just 2 mm thick on average, but it is so important that it receives up to one third of your body's blood supply and has its own special glands (organs that make chemical substances). It is waterproof, protects you against some of the harmful effects of sunlight, and helps keep you at just the right temperature. Skin even helps to nourish you by using sunlight to make vitamin D, and storing water, fat, glucose and vitamin D.

SKIN SANDWICH

Although it's very thin, your skin is complicated. It has three main layers. The outer layer is made mostly of dead skin, and is called the epidermis (1). Beneath this, the dermis (2) contains all the glands and makes new skin cells. The innermost layer is mostly fat, and is called the hypodermis (3).

▶ Like apes and monkeys, we have a nail on the end of each of our fingers and toes. Nails are like the claws of other animals.

Skin is thinnest on your eyelids, at just **0.5 mm** thick, and thickest on the soles of your feet, where it is **6 mm** thick.

Nail root
Cuticle
Nail bed
Nail
Bone
Fat

▲ Nails grow about 3 mm in a month, and grow fastest in summer.

NAILED IT

Nails are made from a tough material called keratin. They are mostly dead cells, except at the nail root where they are made, and the nail bed where they slide along the fingertip. As they grow, each whole nail is pushed along towards the tip of your finger.

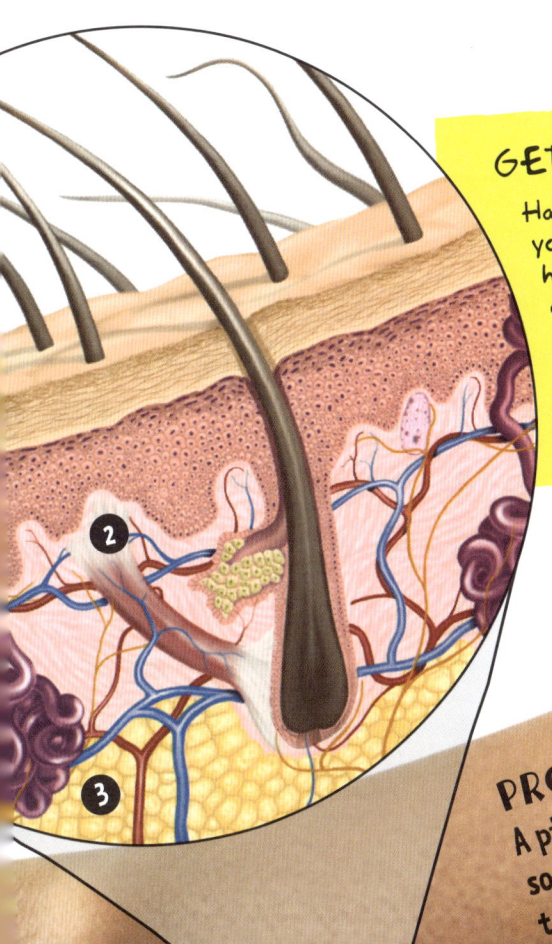

GETTING HAIRY

Hair is the fastest-growing thing on your body. You have about 100,000 hairs on your head, all growing about one centimetre per month, and hot weather makes them grow faster! People with fair hair have lots more hairs than those with red hair – 150,000 to a redhead's 90,000.

PROTECTIVE COATING

A pigment called melanin gives your skin some protection against the effects of too much sunlight. Skin colour depends on the type and amount of melanin pigments in your skin – lighter skin has less and darker skin has more.

How do wounds heal?

First, platelet cells rush to the wound to make blood **clot** (thicken and stick together).

Next, other special blood cells (white) arrive to fight **infection**.

Then material in the blood called **fibrin** (yellow) forms a fibrous mesh. Platelets and red blood cells are trapped. They form a jelly-like mass, which dries to form a **scab**, and the skin heals underneath.

Sun stoppers

Too much sun can damage your skin. Find out how well suntan lotions protect it with this simple test.

SUPPLIES

masking tape • scissors • transparent plastic folders • two or more sunscreens with the same protection factor • tray • sunprint paper kit tub or basin of water

HOW TO MAKE

1. Stick the masking tape in a simple pattern onto the plastic folders (one for each lotion).

2. Smear a different sunscreen onto each folder. Label them so you can identify them.

3. Place one folder on a flat tray, slide a sheet of sunprint paper into it, take the tray out into the sun, and leave in direct sunlight for two minutes (or according to your kit's instructions).

4. Bring the tray back out of the sun, take the paper out of the folder and immerse in water for one minute (or according to kit instructions), then lay flat to dry.

5. Repeat steps 3 and 4 for all your folders.

6. Check the strength of the patterns on the prints: the weakest pattern indicates the strongest sun protection.

109

Airbags

Every cell in your body needs a continual supply of oxygen – especially those in your brain. That's why your body has an incredible system for taking oxygen from the air when you breathe in, and why you would die if you stopped breathing.

BREATHTAKING

Inside your chest, you have two lungs. Each lung is a spongy bag packed full of tiny branching airways, like an upside down tree. When you breathe in, your lungs inflate like balloons to draw air in through your nose and mouth and down your trachea (windpipe). Scientists call breathing 'respiration'.

▶ Your lungs take oxygen from the air into the blood vessels that surround them so that it can be pumped around your body by your heart.

Windpipe

Lung

BREATH POWER

Your blood delivers energy to your cells in the form of a sugary chemical called glucose. In the same way that a fire needs oxygen to burn, so your cells need oxygen to release the energy from glucose. The process releases carbon dioxide, which your body expels as you breathe out, because it is poisonous.

◀ When you run fast, your muscles need extra oxygen, so your lungs must work hard to take in more air.

Model lungs

Make you own working model of your lungs and diaphragm!

SUPPLIES
empty plastic water bottle • craft knife
biodegradable balloon • plastic bag • scissors
elastic band

HOW TO MAKE
1. Ask an adult to help you cut the top half off the bottle, keeping your cut straight. This will be your chest cavity.

2. Slip a balloon over the bottle's nozzle and push the balloon upside down firmly into the bottleneck. This is your lung.

3. Cut a square from the plastic bag that will cover the cut end of your bottle with a few centimetres to spare all round.

4. Place the plastic over the cut end of the bottle and secure with the elastic band. This is your diaphragm.

HOW TO USE
Pinch the diaphragm plastic between your fingers and push firmly up inside the bottle. What happens to the lung balloon?

Pull the diaphragm plastic out to its fullest extent. Now what happens?

You should see the lung balloon inflate and deflate, as your lungs do when your diaphragm pulls.

Bronchi
At the bottom of the windpipe, the airways fork into two large pipes called bronchi, one leading to each lung.

Bronchiole
Inside the lung, the bronchi branch into tens of thousands of narrower pipes called bronchioles. At the end of each bronchiole are bunches of air sacs called alveoli.

▶ The alveoli are like a bunch of tiny balloons. It takes just seconds for oxygen to seep through their thin walls and into the blood vessels that are wrapped around them.

Heart

Diaphragm
When you breathe in, your chest muscles and diaphragm (a large sheet of muscle beneath the lungs) pull out to make the lungs expand. When you breathe out, the muscles relax to let the lungs collapse like a deflated balloon.

It's a gas

① You breathe in air containing oxygen (O_2) and other gases.

② In the lungs, O_2 is taken into the bloodstream.

③ O_2 is carried away in the blood.

④ Blood carries carbon dioxide (CO_2) back to the lungs.

⑤ CO_2 is carried out of the body as you breathe out.

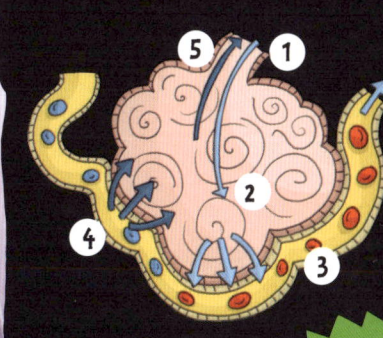

Pump it!

Your heart is a pump that pushes blood around your body. It beats away inside your chest to keep blood constantly circulating. No cell in your body can survive long without the array of chemicals delivered in the blood.

BLOOD ON THE MOVE

One side of your heart pumps blood around your body through a branching network of tubes called blood vessels. It pumps bright-red blood rich in fresh oxygen away from the lungs through vessels called arteries. Once it has delivered its oxygen, the blood turns purple and returns to the heart through blood vessels called veins.

▶ The red arteries and blue veins are like two similar branching trees of blood vessels, meeting at your heart.

Your heart beats about 70 times a minute and over **30 million times** each year. When you exert yourself, it beats **even faster**.

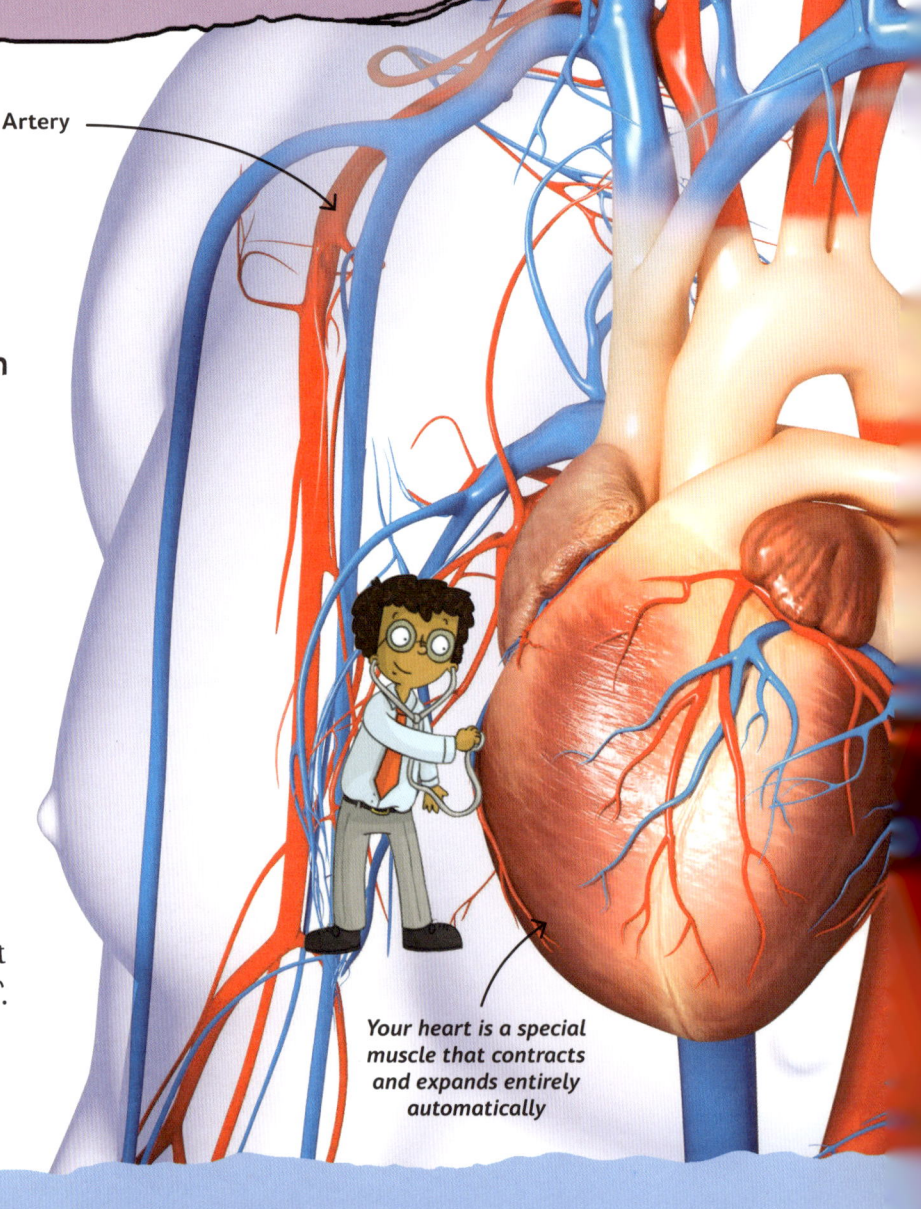

Artery

Your heart is a special muscle that contracts and expands entirely automatically

Blood groups

Your blood is one of four main 'groups'. If you are injured and need to be given blood, you must receive blood from the right group, as your **immune system** may fight against blood from the wrong group.

The most common blood group is O. Blood from this group can be given safely to any other group. People with this blood type are known as '**universal** donors'.

The other **three** main blood groups are A, B and AB.

CIRCULATION

Blood circulation has two parts. Pulmonary circulation carries blood through the lungs. Systemic circulation pushes blood from the heart all around the body. The heart's weaker right side pumps the pulmonary circulation. Its strong left side pumps the systemic circulation. Each side has two chambers: an atrium to collect blood, and a ventricle to pump the blood on.

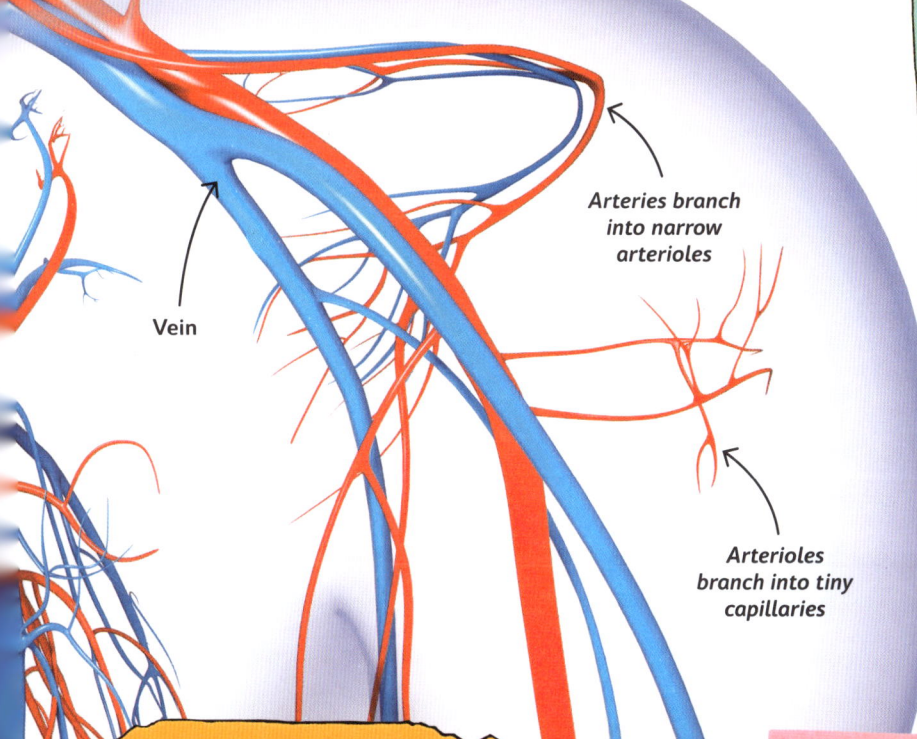

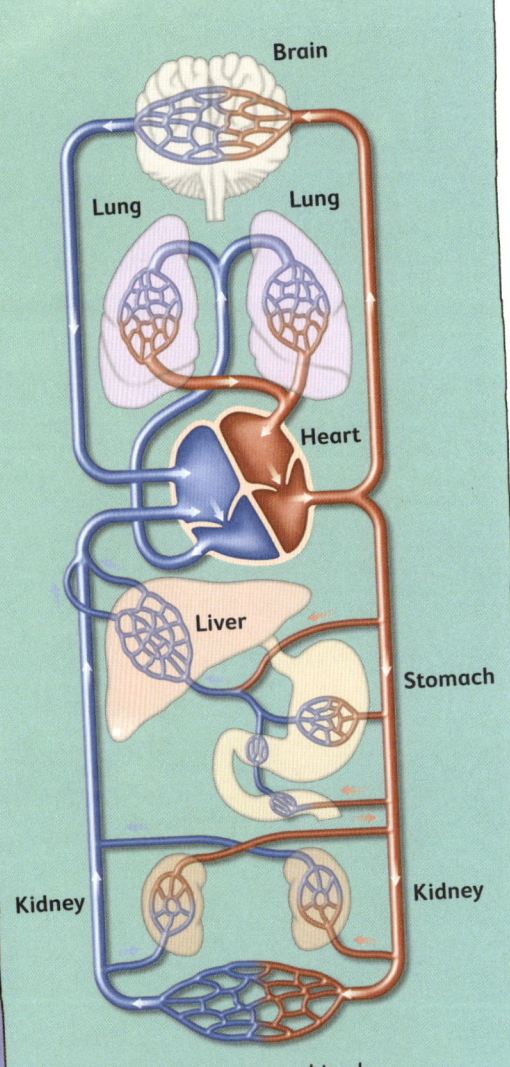

Vein

Arteries branch into narrow arterioles

Arterioles branch into tiny capillaries

Brain
Lung
Lung
Heart
Liver
Stomach
Kidney
Kidney

▲ This diagram shows the two parts of blood circulation. Blood rich in oxygen is red, deoxygenated blood is blue.

Listen to the beat

Doctors sometimes listen to your chest using a device called a stethoscope. Here's how to make a simple stethoscope to listen to your heart beating.

SUPPLIES
1 m of broad plastic tubing • plastic funnel

HOW TO MAKE
Insert the neck of the funnel into one end of the tube.

HOW TO USE
1. Hold the mouth of the funnel against your chest, slightly to your left. This is where your heart is. Put the other end of the tube against your ear and listen hard. You should hear your heart beating.

2. Run on the spot for a few minutes, then listen to your heart again – it should be beating faster.

113

Down the hatch

When you swallow food, it begins a long journey down through your gut. On its way, it is gradually broken down into chemical molecules small enough for your body to absorb and use. This breakdown process is called digestion.

THE FOOD TUBE

Your gut is a very long tube that curls through your body between your mouth and your anus, around 10 m long. It's also called the alimentary canal and runs down through your gullet, your stomach, your small intestine and your large intestine.

Your stomach can swell up to **eight times** as big when it is full.

1 Your stomach is a bag-like organ, and it's where the breakdown of food really begins. Chemicals inside it attack the food, and the walls squeeze it to a pulp. Your stomach also stores partially digested food until the rest of the gut is ready to receive it.

Your stomach produces hydrochloric **acid** strong enough to dissolve a lump of bone in a few hours. That's why your stomach lining is coated with protective mucus.

Enzyme breakdown

Biological soap powders use special chemicals called enzymes to clean dirt proteins on clothes. You can use them to see how enzymes in your digestive system break down proteins in food.

SUPPLIES
jam • teaspoon • two strips of white cotton • small amount of biological soap power with enzymes and non-biological soap powder without enzymes • two small dishes • water

HOW TO MAKE

1. Smear a patch of jam on each cotton strip and let them dry.

2. Mix a little of each soap in separate dishes with the same amount of water.

3. Dip the jammy part of one cotton strip into the dish containing the soap with enzymes and the other into the one without.

4. Leave the strips for half an hour. You should find the jam has almost gone from the strip in the enzyme dish. The enzymes break up the proteins in jam in the same way as enzymes in your gut break down proteins in food.

Oesophagus

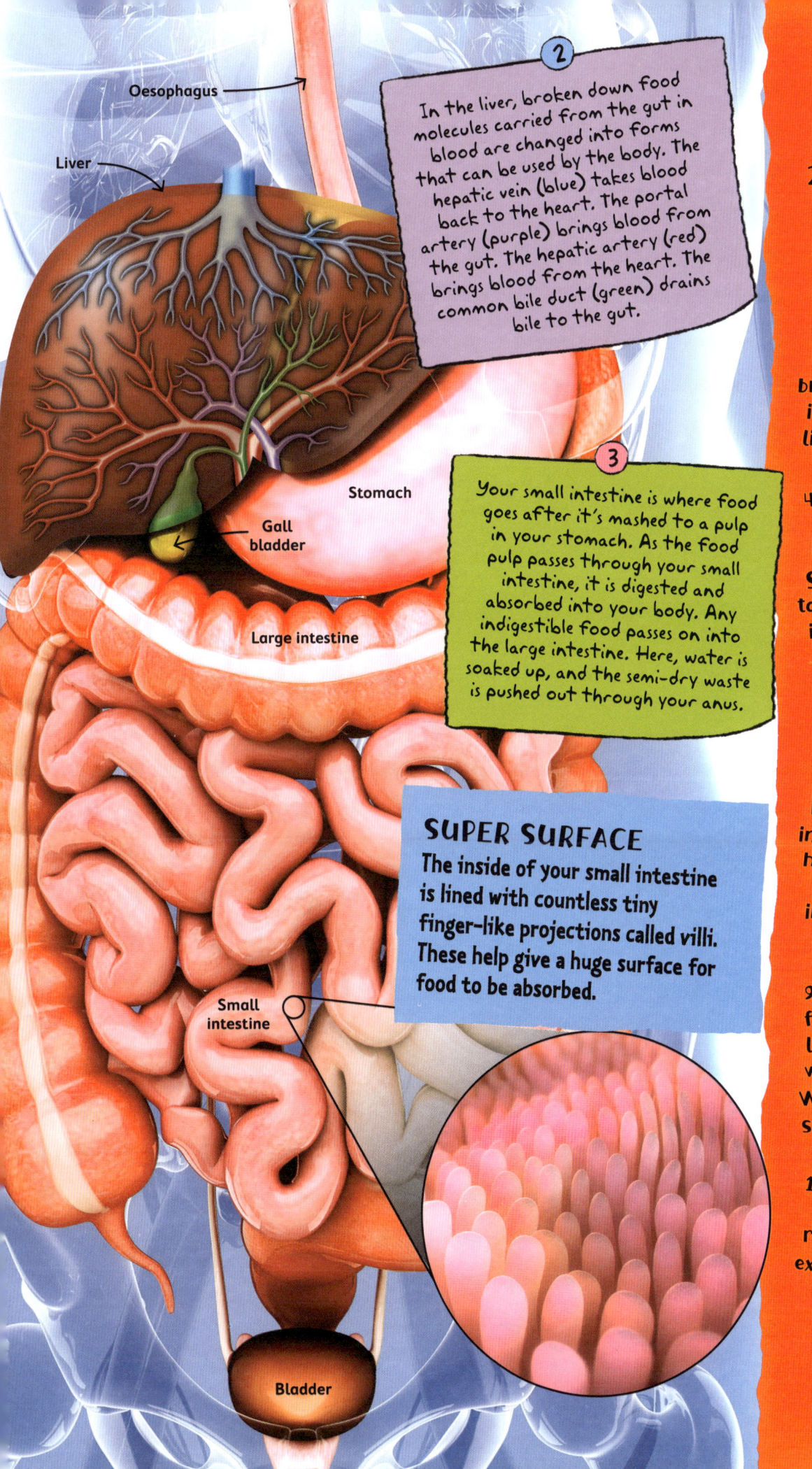

Liver

Stomach

Gall bladder

Large intestine

Small intestine

Bladder

2 In the liver, broken down food molecules carried from the gut in blood are changed into forms that can be used by the body. The hepatic vein (blue) takes blood back to the heart. The portal artery (purple) brings blood from the gut. The hepatic artery (red) brings blood from the heart. The common bile duct (green) drains bile to the gut.

3 Your small intestine is where food goes after it's mashed to a pulp in your stomach. As the food pulp passes through your small intestine, it is digested and absorbed into your body. Any indigestible food passes on into the large intestine. Here, water is soaked up, and the semi-dry waste is pushed out through your anus.

SUPER SURFACE
The inside of your small intestine is lined with countless tiny finger-like projections called villi. These help give a huge surface for food to be absorbed.

Digestion timeline

Food takes up to **24 hours** to pass through the gut.

0 hours: When you **swallow** food, it slides down to the stomach where it is broken down into semi-liquid form.

4 hours: Partially digested food passes from the **stomach** to the small intestine.

7 hours: Broken down food molecules are absorbed into the **bloodstream** in the second half of the small intestine.

9 hours: Undigested food passes into the large intestine where any **water** is soaked up.

17–24 hours: Waste passes into the rectum and is then excreted up to **two days** later.

115

Water works

Besides food and air, your body needs water. You cannot survive more than a few days without it. Your body is more than 60 percent water, and the balance of water is crucial to your survival.

HOLDING WATER

When your body has too little water, the concentration of chemicals in your blood goes up. A special organ in your brain called the hypothalamus detects this, and sends a signal to another organ called the pituitary gland. The pituitary releases a chemical called ADH, which tells your kidneys to let less water escape as urine in order to restore the balance.

▶ When you sweat to keep cool, your brain's hypothalamus (1) detects the water loss and tells the pituitary gland (2) to send out thirst signals.

Water balance

The amount of water in your body must never vary by more than **five percent**. Constant adjustments — taking water in and letting it out — keep the balance just right.

Input	Litres
Drinks	1.2
Food	1
From body cells	0.3
TOTAL	2.5

Output	Litres
Urine	1.5
Sweat	0.5
Vapour in breath	0.3
Faeces	0.2
TOTAL	2.5

FANTASTIC FILTERS

The main way you lose water is through urine, which is controlled by your kidneys. Your kidneys filter unwanted water from the blood and flush out waste chemicals. The waste water is then piped as urine into your bladder. There the pressure of liquid builds up until you urinate.

▶ Every day, your kidneys filter 150 l of blood and extract about 1.5 l of urine, which they expel through the ureter.

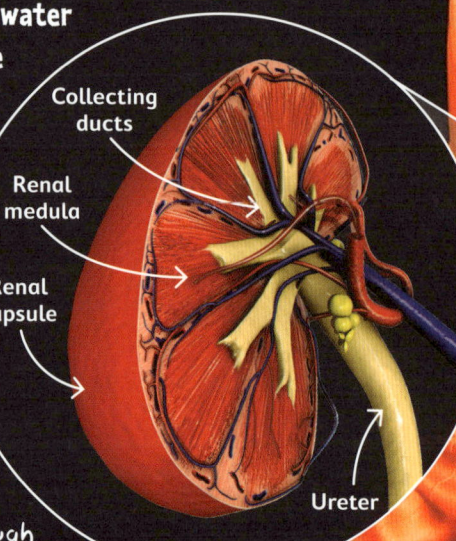

- Collecting ducts
- Renal medula
- Renal capsule
- Ureter

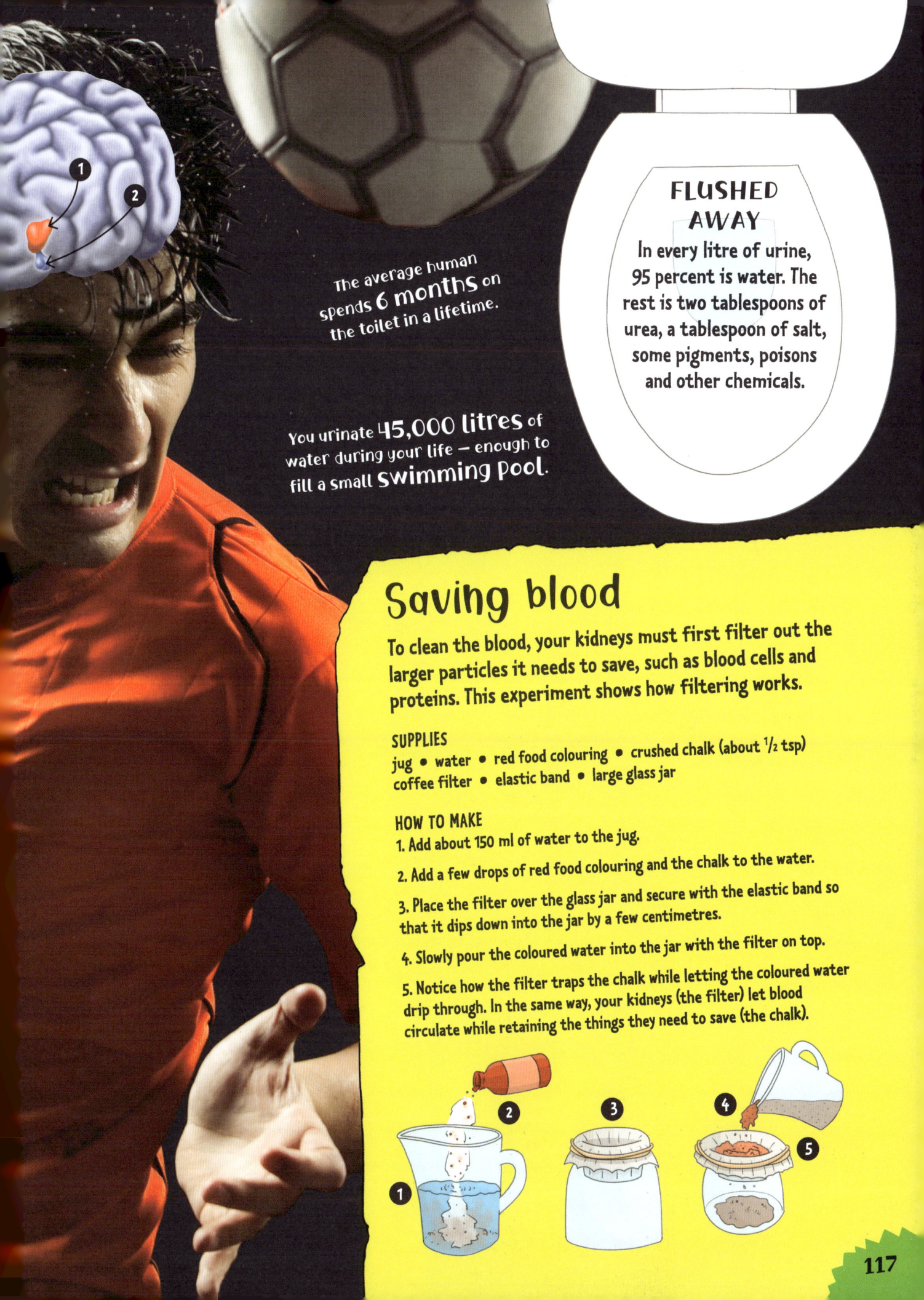

The average human spends **6 months** on the toilet in a lifetime.

You urinate **45,000 litres** of water during your life – enough to fill a small **swimming pool**.

FLUSHED AWAY
In every litre of urine, 95 percent is water. The rest is two tablespoons of urea, a tablespoon of salt, some pigments, poisons and other chemicals.

Saving blood

To clean the blood, your kidneys must first filter out the larger particles it needs to save, such as blood cells and proteins. This experiment shows how filtering works.

SUPPLIES
jug • water • red food colouring • crushed chalk (about ½ tsp)
coffee filter • elastic band • large glass jar

HOW TO MAKE
1. Add about 150 ml of water to the jug.

2. Add a few drops of red food colouring and the chalk to the water.

3. Place the filter over the glass jar and secure with the elastic band so that it dips down into the jar by a few centimetres.

4. Slowly pour the coloured water into the jar with the filter on top.

5. Notice how the filter traps the chalk while letting the coloured water drip through. In the same way, your kidneys (the filter) let blood circulate while retaining the things they need to save (the chalk).

Pulling together

Every move you make depends on muscles. You need them to go for a walk, chew your food, and even when you're fast asleep. Without them you'd just collapse like a puppet with its strings cut.

MUSCLE TYPES
You have two main kinds of muscles. Skeletal (voluntary) muscles cover your skeleton and allow you to move. Involuntary muscles work automatically to control body functions, such as your heartbeat.

▶ Almost all of your 640 skeletal muscles are attached to your skeleton. They produce movement and give your body its shape.

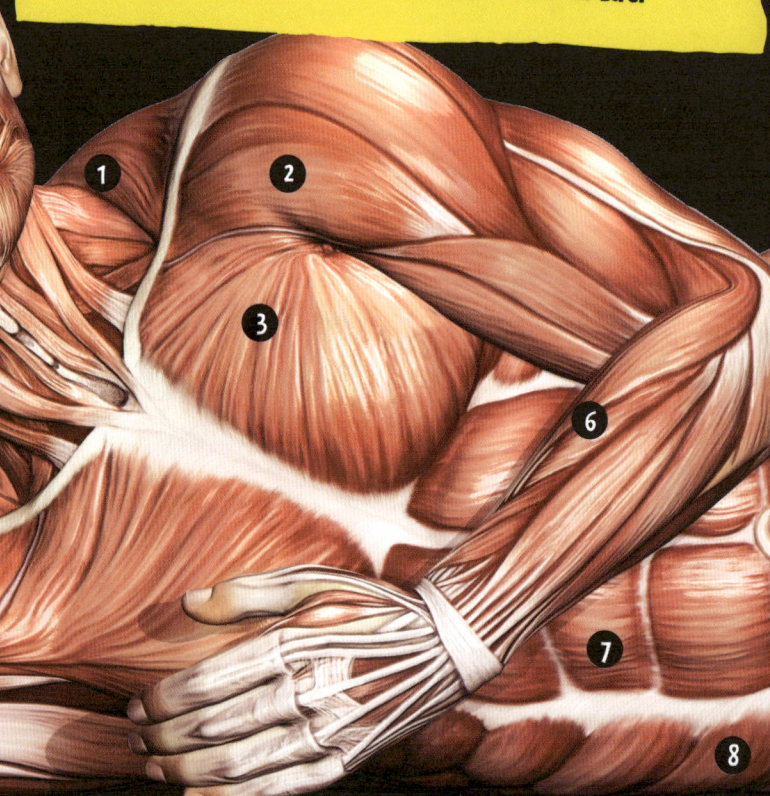

Too cool!

The strongest muscle in your body is the masseter muscle in your **cheeks** that make you bite. Your tongue is a close second.

The smallest muscle is less than 1.3 mm long. It's called the stapedius and is in your **inner ear**.

The largest muscles are made from **hundreds** of bundles of muscle fibre.

The biggest muscle is in your **bum**. It's called the gluteus maximus and gets its name from the Greek and Latin words for 'bum' and 'biggest'.

118

POWER CONTRACT

Muscles get their power from bundles of fibres that contract and relax. Inside each fibre are alternating, interlocking filaments of two substances called actin and myosin. These pull and twist into each other to shorten the muscle whenever they get a signal from the brain.

▶ This microscope picture shows a slice across the tiny fibres of a muscle that give it its pulling power.

WORKING IN PAIRS

A single muscle can only pull, not push. So each time one muscle contracts, it must be pulled back to its original length by another muscle shortening in the opposite direction. This is why muscles are usually arranged in pairs.

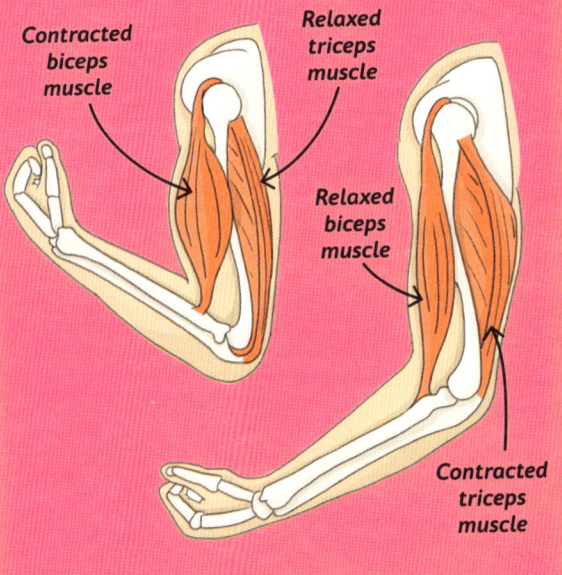

Contracted biceps muscle
Relaxed triceps muscle
Relaxed biceps muscle
Contracted triceps muscle

▲ The biceps and triceps muscles in your upper arm work in conjunction to pull your forearm one way then the other.

MUSCLES OF THE ARMS AND TORSO

1 Trapezius
2 Deltoid
3 Pectoralis
4 Biceps
5 Triceps
6 Brachioradialis
7 Rectus abodominis
8 External oblique abdominal

MUSCLES OF THE LEGS

9 Adductors
10 Pectineus
11 Tensor fasciae latae
12 Sartorius
13 Rectus femoris
14 Vastus lateralis
15 Vastus medialis
16 Tibialis anterior
17 Gastrocnemius
18 Soleus

If all the muscles in your body **pulled together** they could lift a bus!

119

Super skeleton

Bones give your body a strong, rigid but remarkably light framework called the skeleton. It's the one part of your body that remains long after you die, yet while you're alive, it is living tissue.

All about joints

Swivel joints in the neck allow the head to rotate.

The **saddle** joint allows your thumb to move in two directions.

Ellipsoidal joints, found at the base of the first finger and in the toes, allow movement in various directions.

Ball-and-socket joints, found in the hip and shoulder, allow circular movement.

Hinge joints, like those in the elbow and knee, allow a swinging movement to and fro.

Plane joints in the wrists and ankles allow smooth circular and bending movements.

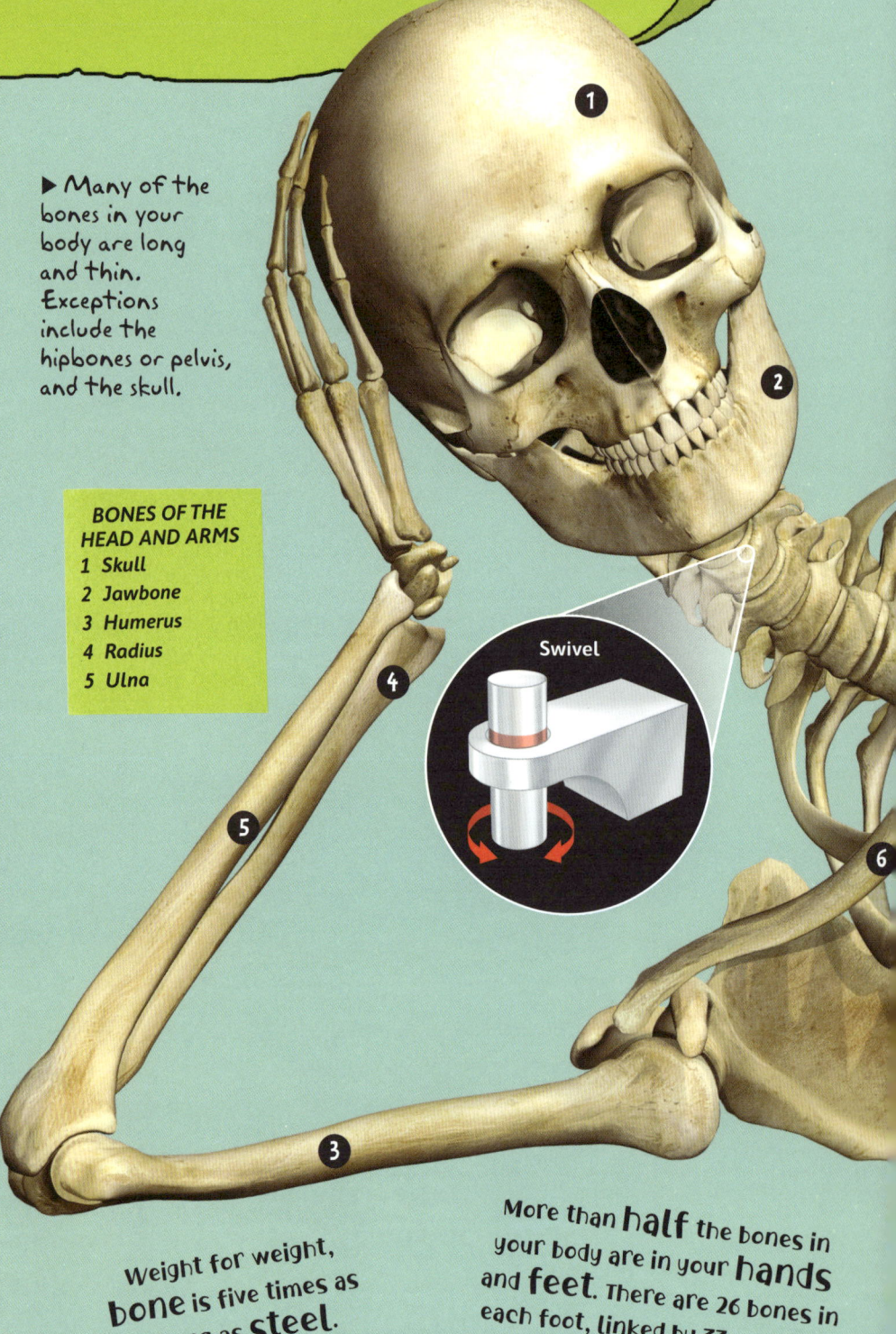

▶ Many of the bones in your body are long and thin. Exceptions include the hipbones or pelvis, and the skull.

BONES OF THE HEAD AND ARMS
1 Skull
2 Jawbone
3 Humerus
4 Radius
5 Ulna

Swivel

Weight for weight, **bone** is five times as strong as **steel**.

More than **half** the bones in your body are in your **hands** and **feet**. There are 26 bones in each foot, linked by 33 muscles.

120

LIVING BONES

Inside, bones are packed with cells called osteocytes between a framework of hard minerals. Flexible collagen fibres and stiff honeycomb-like struts called trabeculae criss-cross, forming a super-strong combination.

▶ Bone has a hard 'cortex' of compact bone encasing spongy 'cancellous' bone. In the middle is a soft core or marrow.

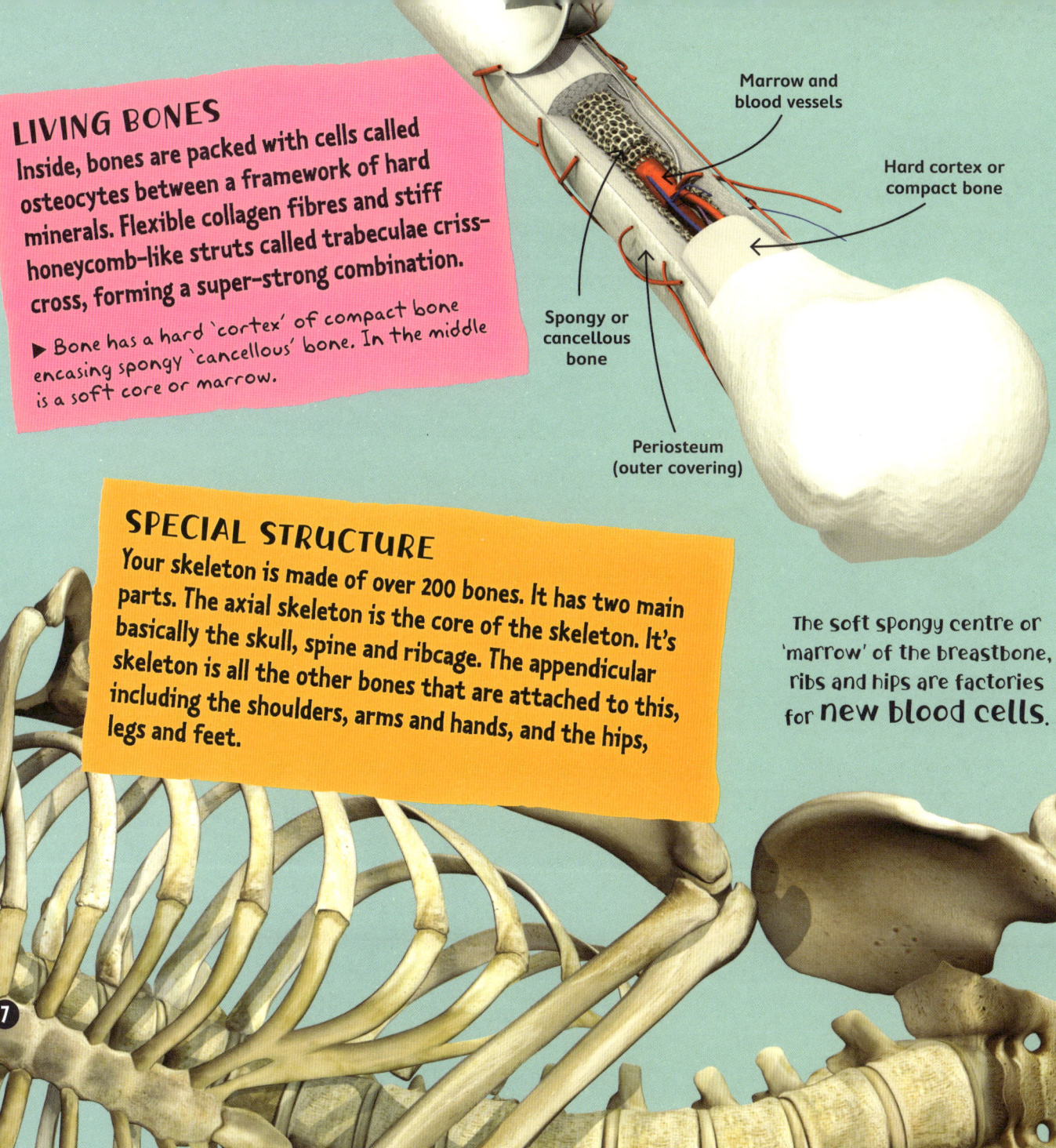

Marrow and blood vessels
Hard cortex or compact bone
Spongy or cancellous bone
Periosteum (outer covering)

SPECIAL STRUCTURE

Your skeleton is made of over 200 bones. It has two main parts. The axial skeleton is the core of the skeleton. It's basically the skull, spine and ribcage. The appendicular skeleton is all the other bones that are attached to this, including the shoulders, arms and hands, and the hips, legs and feet.

The soft spongy centre or 'marrow' of the breastbone, ribs and hips are factories for **new blood cells**.

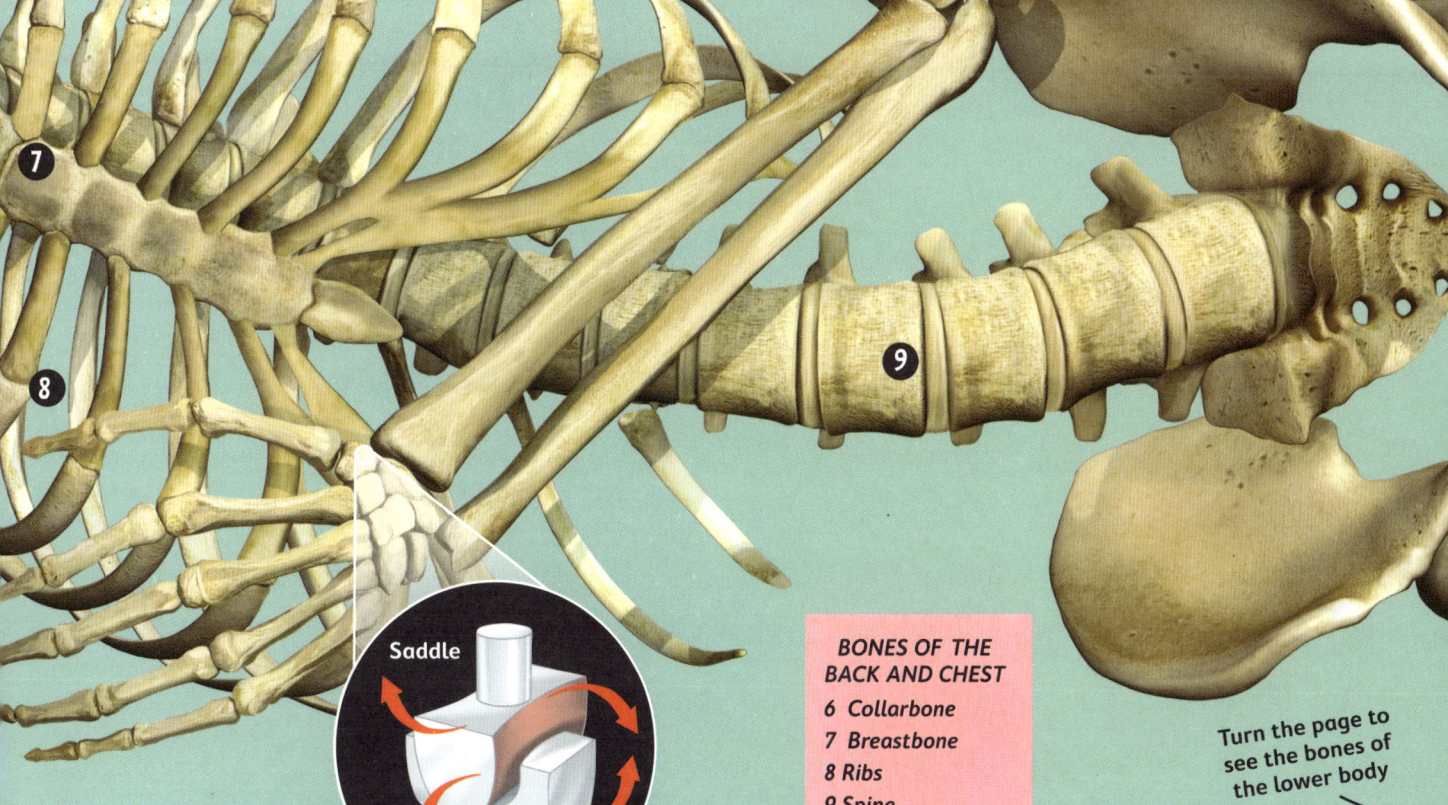

Saddle

BONES OF THE BACK AND CHEST
6 Collarbone
7 Breastbone
8 Ribs
9 Spine

Turn the page to see the bones of the lower body

121

Bone idol

Our bones are very special. Our skeleton is so light it accounts for only 14 percent of total body weight, yet bone can stand being squeezed twice as hard as granite and being stretched four times as hard as concrete.

▶ A gymnast's muscles pull the bones to which they are anchored so that they can perform a range of movements requiring supreme flexibility, balance, control and strength.

Ball-and-socket

JOINT ENTERPRISE

The skeleton is strong and rigid, yet can bend pretty much any way you want. That's because it's made of lots of separate bones linked only by movable joints. Here, the bones are held together by fibres called ligaments and cushioned by smooth, rubbery cartilage.

BONES OF THE HIP AND LEGS
1 Hip bone
2 Thigh bone
3 Kneecap
4 Shinbone
5 Calf bone

There are 80 bones in the axial skeleton and 126 bones in the appendicular skeleton.

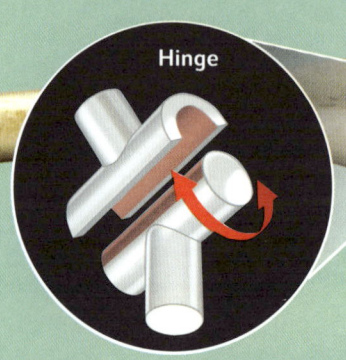

Hinge

Bones get their rigidity from hard deposits of minerals such as **calcium** and **phosphate**.

◀ Calcar's drawings showed intricate details of anatomy, often in poses like this one, which shows a skeleton as if relaxing against a tomb.

BROKEN BONES
Sometimes, despite their strength, bones do get broken or 'fractured'. Fortunately, most fractures heal. First, the body stops any bleeding, then gradually the fracture is knitted together with new bone by osteoblasts. But surgeons may need to straighten the break out and hold it in place with pins or a plaster cast to ensure the bone repairs itself in the right way.

STUDYING THE SKELETON
The first accurate drawings of the skeleton were made by Johannes Stephanus of Calcar in the 1540s. He drew the bones of bodies carefully dissected (cut up) by the famous Belgian physician Andre Vesalius. The skeleton Vesalius prepared can still be seen in Basel in Switzerland.

▲ When bones break this badly, they must be realigned by surgery to heal properly.

Bones **grow** by getting longer near the end, at a region called the **epiphyseal plate**.

The word 'skeleton' comes from the **ancient Greek** word for dry.

Ellipsoidal

Plane

123

Brilliant brain

If you could see your brain, you might say it looks like a giant soggy grey walnut. But it's actually the most amazing structure, containing hundreds of billions of nerve cells, some of them linked to 25,000 or more others, creating trillions of connections.

INSIDE YOUR BRAIN

Your brain is 85 percent water and quite a lot of fat. But what really matters is the nerve cells held in tight bundles by supporting glial cells. The brain is split into two hemispheres, linked by a bundle of nerves. Scientists can learn about the brain by studying MRI scans – images made using strong magnetic fields to show details of brain structure and activity.

▶ The inside of your brain is much more than just a dense mat of fibres. Inside are a variety of structures, each with its own task.

CORTEX
The wrinkled outer layer is where your brain receives all the sense signals from your body and responds with messages to react.

Where's that letter?

You can test how good your short-term memory is with this simple word game. You can use letters from a set of 'Scrabble' tiles, or you can make your own paper letter tiles.

HOW TO PLAY

1. Select 16 letter tiles – start with ten consonants and six vowels, and make sure you have a good variety of letters.

2. Lay them on a flat surface in a grid, face up. Try to memorize the position of each letter.

3. Turn all the letters face down.

4. Turn one letter face up. Using your memory, see if you can turn over tiles in the right order to form a word of at least three letters.

5. Once you have made a word, try to make second.

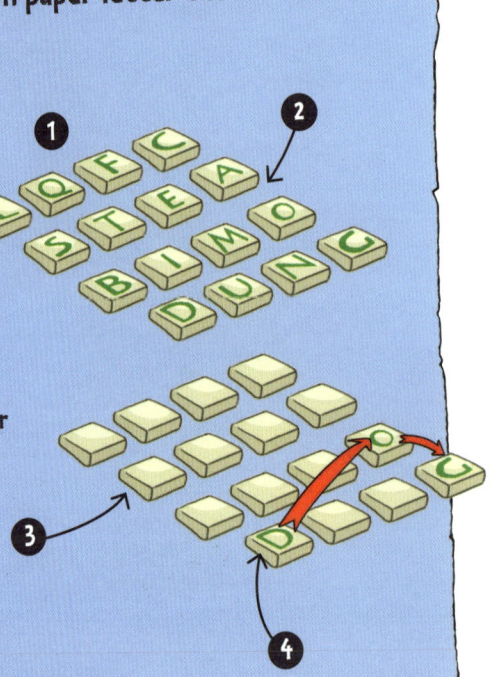

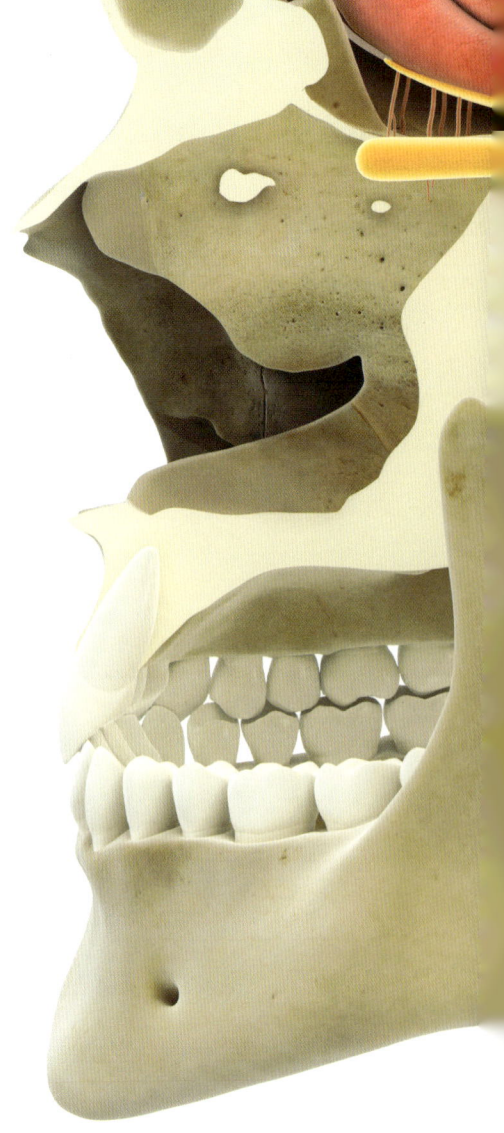

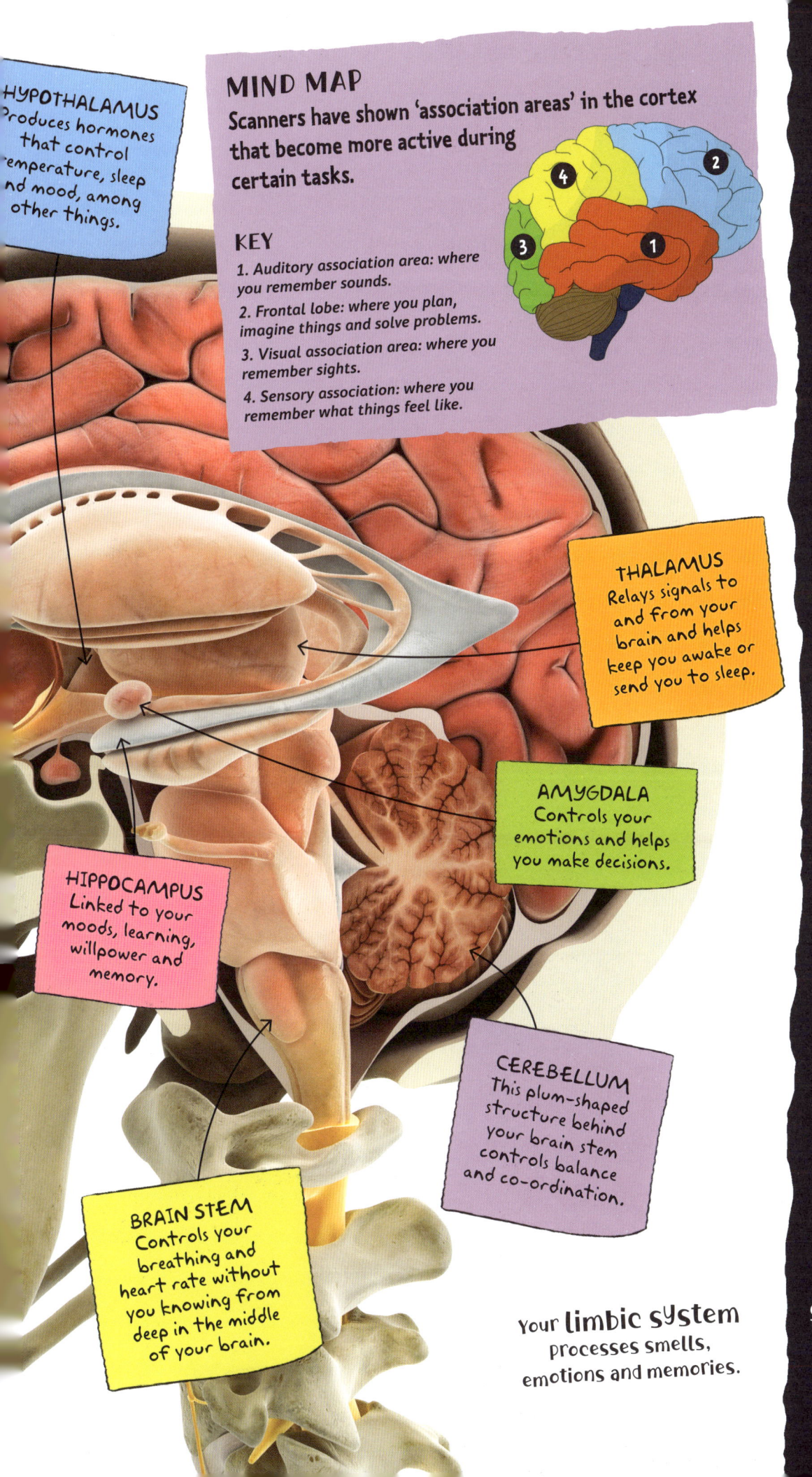

HYPOTHALAMUS Produces hormones that control temperature, sleep and mood, among other things.

MIND MAP
Scanners have shown 'association areas' in the cortex that become more active during certain tasks.

KEY
1. Auditory association area: where you remember sounds.
2. Frontal lobe: where you plan, imagine things and solve problems.
3. Visual association area: where you remember sights.
4. Sensory association: where you remember what things feel like.

THALAMUS Relays signals to and from your brain and helps keep you awake or send you to sleep.

AMYGDALA Controls your emotions and helps you make decisions.

HIPPOCAMPUS Linked to your moods, learning, willpower and memory.

CEREBELLUM This plum-shaped structure behind your brain stem controls balance and co-ordination.

BRAIN STEM Controls your breathing and heart rate without you knowing from deep in the middle of your brain.

Your **limbic system** processes smells, emotions and memories.

I remember

Your brain stores **memories** by making new connections between brain cells. They are made in three stages:

1. Sensory
memory: Your senses continue seeing, hearing or feeling something for a short while after it stops.

2. Short-term
memory: Your brain stores something like a name just long enough to pass it on.

3. Long-term
memory: Your brain makes strong connections so that you remember things for a long time.

3a. Declarative memories are things you remember **consciously**, such as the name of your favourite band or where the supermarket is.

3b. Non-declarative memories are things you remember **subconsciously** such as how to tie your shoelaces.

125

Get the message

Your nervous system is your body's control system. It's like a high-speed internet, with neurons (nerve cells) whizzing messages to and fro. Sensory neurons receive messages from the senses, while motor neurons send messages to the muscles to move.

NERVE CENTRAL

The hub of your nervous system is the bundle of nerves running down your spine, known as the spinal cord. Together with your brain it makes up the Central Nervous System (CNS). More nerves branch out from the CNS all over the body. These nerves are the Peripheral Nervous System (PNS). Sensory neurons transmit nerve impulses from sensory receptors to the CNS. Motor neurones transmit signals from the CNS telling the muscles to move.

CHEMICAL CHANGES

Eating chocolate sets off floods of neurotransmitters (chemicals) such as endorphins and serotonin. These are linked to happy feelings, which may be why people like chocolate!

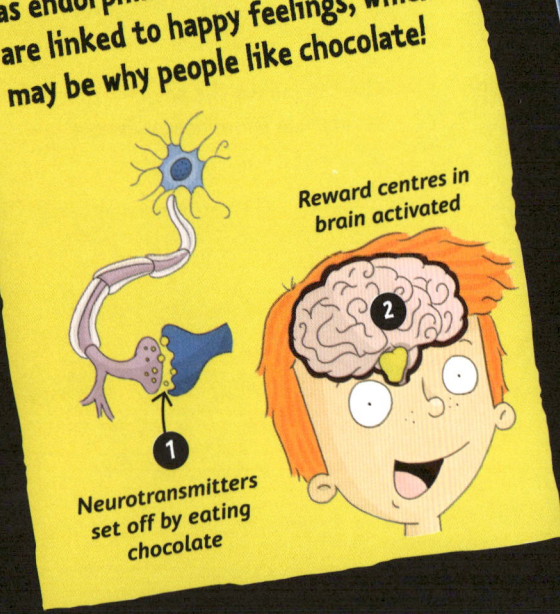

1. Neurotransmitters set off by eating chocolate
2. Reward centres in brain activated

The **fastest** nerve signals travel at 120 m/sec!

- Brain
- Intercostal nerve
- Spinal cord
- Sciatic nerve

▲ Nerves branch out all over the body from the Central Nervous System, which consists of the brain and the spinal cord.

MAKING A CONNECTION
Neurons transmit signals through a combination of electrical and chemical pulses. They receive signals from other neurons through thousands of branching connectors called dendrites. They send signals out via an axon (a long tail) to lots more dendrites, which are linked to other neurons.

After passing a signal, a nerve cell is ready to send another in 0.01 seconds!

Axon terminal of sending neuron

Dendrite of receiving neuron

Synapse

Neurotransmitters

MIND THE GAP
No two nerve cells touch. Instead, they transmit signals across a synapse (a tiny gap), in the form of neurotransmitters (streams of chemical particles). Nerve cells respond in different ways to different neurotransmitters, so these can have a dramatic effect on your mood.

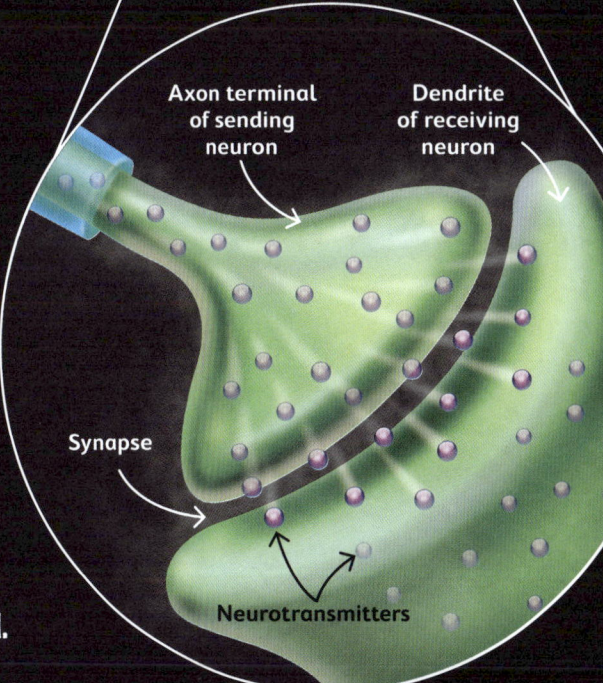

Test your reflexes
Reflex movements are muscle movements in your body that happen without you thinking about them. An alarm signal from a sense neuron goes straight to a motor neuron, cutting your brain out of the process so that your body can react with lightning speed.

HOW IT WORKS
The tap makes the thigh muscle stretch. In 50 milliseconds, the information is sent to the spinal cord, and then comes straight back to the thigh muscle to make it contract and kick out your leg.

HOW TO DO
1. Ask a friend to sit cross-legged so that one leg dangles freely.
2. Tap his or her leg firmly with the side of your hand just below the kneecap.
3. If you hit the right place, your friend's leg will kick out at once.

All eyes

Eyes are sometimes compared to cameras. But their picture quality beats even the best digital cameras. They are also much more versatile than any camera — they can focus on a speck of dust just centimetres away or a galaxy far across the universe, and work in both starlight and sunlight.

EYE EYE
Your eyes are two hollow balls with a round window at the front called the pupil. Each is filled with a jelly-like substance called vitreous humour. Vitreous means glass-like and humour means body fluid.

PICTURE-MAKERS
The cornea of your eye projects a picture into your eye like a mini-camera.

▼ To change focus from a distant object to a near one, your eyes' ciliary muscles pull in, making the lens smaller and fatter. This bends light rays more and is called accommodation.

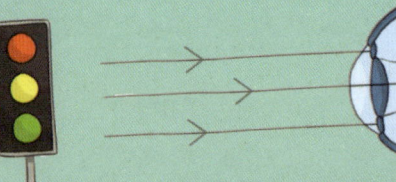

Light rays from a distant object are bent slightly to bring them to focus at the back of the eye

Light rays from nearby objects must be bent more to bring them to focus at the back of the eye

The cornea is a dish-shaped lens at the front of the eye as clear as glass

The pupil looks dark because the eye is dark inside

The iris widens and narrows to control the amount of light entering the eye

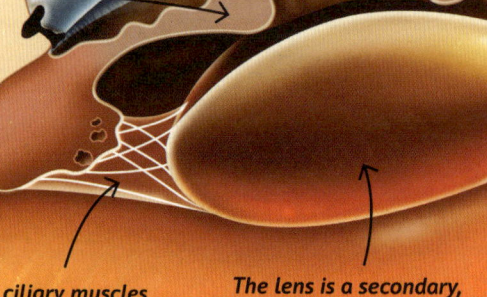

The ciliary muscles adjust the shape of the lens so it can focus at different distances

The lens is a secondary, adjustable lens behind the cornea

▶ The lens (towards the top of this illustration) contains a vast number of cells. Jelly-like vitreous humour in the main body of the eye holds the eye's shape and keeps everything in place.

The optic nerve carries signals from the retina to your brain

128

Make a stereoscope

Our brain combines two pictures – one from each eye – to give us our view of the world. The difference between the angles of the two is what gives everything a solid, 3D look. A simple stereoscopic viewer can mimic this 3D view.

SUPPLIES
digital camera – one on a phone is fine • computer • printer • photoprint paper • scissors • tape • an old shoebox

HOW TO MAKE
1. Support the camera on a table or window ledge, then take a picture.

2. Slide the camera about 10 cm sideways and take a second picture of the same thing.

3. Load the pictures onto a computer and print them. They must be small enough to sit side by side, a few millimetres apart at one end of your box. Cut them out and tape them inside the box, as shown.

4. Cut the lid of the shoebox down to a size where it can form a central divider along the length of your box. Use tape to hold it in place.

5. Cut eyeholes in the box at the opposite end to your pictures.

HOW TO USE
Look through the viewing holes. The two photos will seem to merge, giving your brain the impression that you are looking at a single 3D object. You may need to experiment with how far away from your eyes you hold the box, to find the right position.

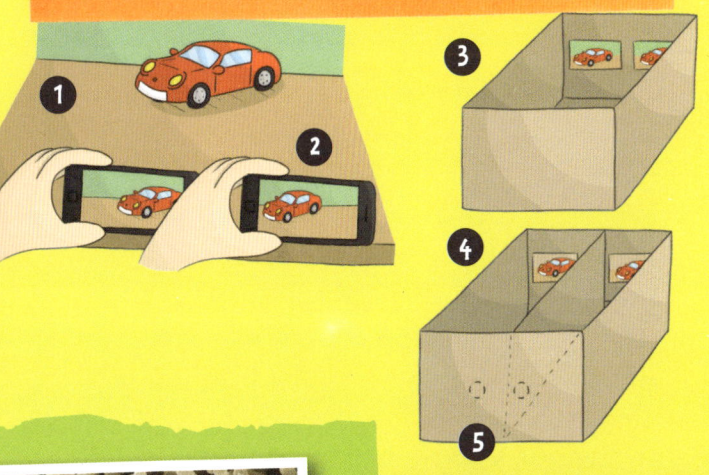

When light hits the retina, the rods and cones send nerve signals down the optic nerve to the visual cortex in the brain, creating your own private movie in your head.

The retina is a mass of light sensor cells that carpet the back of the eye

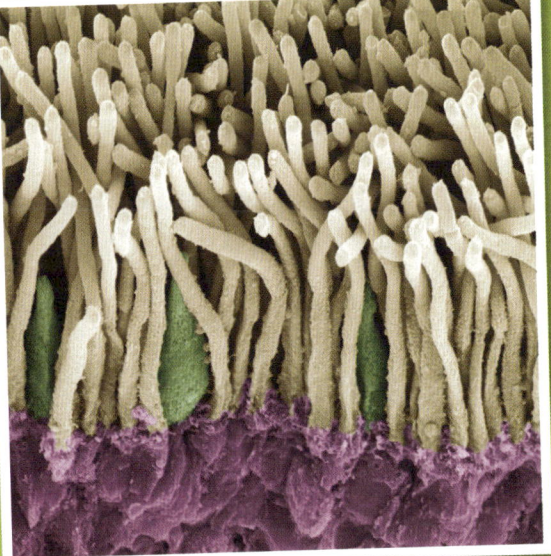

▲ This hugely magnified picture shows the rods (white) and cones (green) in the eye's retina.

YOUR OWN CAMERA

The picture in your eye is millimetres across, yet seems so big and real you never think of it as a picture. The retina that picks it up is like an array of photocells. 'Rods' – 130 million of them – detect if it's dark or light, and work even in low light; 8 million 'cones' detect colours and work best in daylight.

Too cool!

You blink 10–24 times a minute – that's **415 million** times in a lifetime.

Your eyes can tell the difference between **8 million** different colours.

You have **200 eyelashes** on each eye to protect them from dust.

The **iris** is what gives you the **colour** of your eyes.

129

Sound system

Your ears are fantastically sensitive devices for picking up the tiny vibrations in the air that make sound. Your pinnae (ear flaps) are just the funnels to send the vibrations on to the pick-up devices inside your head.

EAR WE GO
Your ear has three sections. The outer ear is the ear flap and ear canal (the tunnel into your head), where sounds are collected. In the middle ear, sound waves are turned into vibrations. The inner ear is where the vibrations are detected.

Super sound waves

Here's a simple project to show how sounds affect your ears so that you hear them.

SUPPLIES
cling film • large bowl • uncooked rice (any other small grain will work) • biscuit tin lid (or other noise maker)

HOW TO MAKE
1. Stretch the cling film tightly over the bowl to make your ear drum model.

2. Scatter some rice grains on the cling film.

3. Firmly hold the tin lid close to your 'ear drum' and bang the lid with your hand. Watch the rice grains move and even jump.

HOW IT WORKS
The bang generates sound waves that make the plastic sheet vibrate and causes the rice grains to move. Sound waves vibrate the eardrum in much the same way.

▶ Every sound you hear is funnelled down the ear canal into the mechanism of the middle and then inner ear. The middle ear turns the changes in air pressure made by sound waves into vibrations that can be detected by your aural (hearing) nerves.

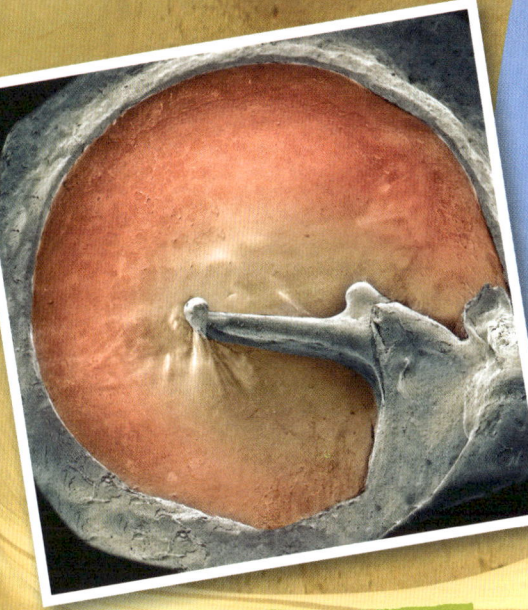

BANG THE DRUM

In your middle ear, sounds hit the eardrum (a thin wall of skin), causing it to vibrate. As it vibrates it rattles the ossicles (three tiny bones), amplifying the vibration.

◀ The pink in this microscope picture shows the eardrum from the inside. The hammer bone is just touching it.

PASS IT ALONG

The vibration in the ossicles starts with the hammer (1). This shakes the anvil (2) so it bangs against the stirrup (3). The stirrup then knocks against the cochlea (4) – a fluid-filled tube shaped like a snail's shell.

▶ The vibration of the ossicles creates waves in the fluid inside the cochlea. The waves waggle hairs that are attached to nerves that tell your brain about the sound.

Eardrum

STEADY!

Your ears are what stop you falling over. Next to the cochlea is a cluster of three fluid-filled rings called semi-circular canals. These canals act like tiny spirit levels, telling you when you're tilting one way or another as the fluid moves inside the canal.

▶ A climber's balance depends on a combination of the fluid-filled canals in his ears and sensors in joints and muscles all over his body.

Too cool!

Your ears have **2000 glands** for making ear wax!

Every day, new ear wax pushes forward the old. It dries up and falls out in tiny clumps or flakes all the time – while you talk, eat, even **sleep**.

You can hear a wider range of sounds than an **owl**, but a narrower range than a **cow**.

Your ears can just hear the lowest notes on a church organ. **Elephants** can hear even deeper sounds.

131

Super senses

Your senses tell you all about the world. Besides sight and sound, there are taste, touch and smell, and a host of other sensations from receptors all over your body.

▶ Your brain uses nerve signals from a range of sensors to experience flavours. These sensors include taste buds in your tongue, aroma sensors in your nose, and others that detect qualities like texture and solidity.

UP YOUR NOSE

The olfactory cells in your nose work in much the same way as taste buds, but instead of five basic types, there are 350 or so! Different aromas stimulate different combinations of smell cells. The average person can identify over 10,000 smells.

Proprioceptors are sensors in joints and muscles all over your body that tell your brain about your **position** and **posture**. That's how you can touch your nose, even with your eyes closed.

WHAT A MOUTHFUL!

A food's flavour doesn't just depend on which of the taste buds in your tongue it triggers. It is also affected by its smell, its texture and even how it looks! And not everyone tastes the same food the same way.

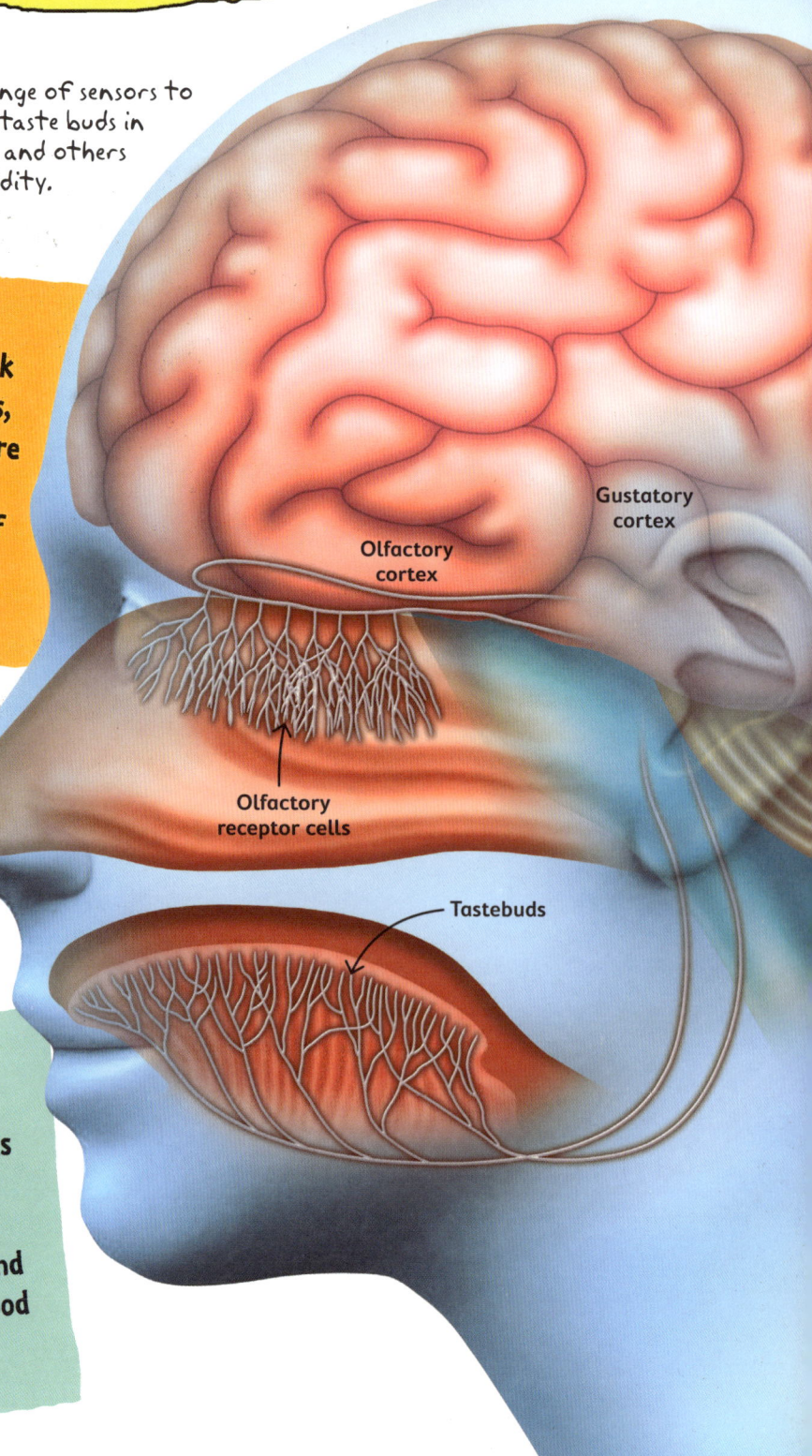

- Gustatory cortex
- Olfactory cortex
- Olfactory receptor cells
- Tastebuds

Test your taste

Have you ever wondered why things don't taste of much when you have a cold? When your nose is stuffed up very little of the smell of your food can reach your olfactory centre. This test shows what a difference your nose makes to what you can taste.

SUPPLIES
apple • potato • table knife
other fruits/vegetables

HOW TO DO
1. Cut an apple and a potato into small pieces of the same size.
2. Close your eyes, pinch your nose to block it, and lick one of the pieces. Can you tell what it is?
3. Try the other piece next.
4. Unblock your nose and try again. How do they taste now?
5. Try the same test for other foods.

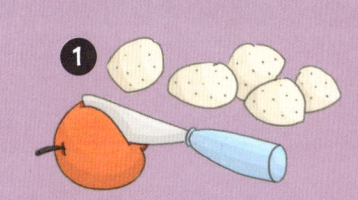

TASTE CELLS

The red dots you can see on the front of your tongue are called papillae. They contain receptors called taste buds. Food dissolved in saliva washes into them and into contact with the receptors.

▶ This microscope picture of the surface of the tongue shows the papillae in pink.

Too cool!

Girls detect smells better than **boys**.

Your tongue can taste a **single drop** of lemon juice mixed in with 129,000 drops of water.

Your tongue has 8000 taste buds.

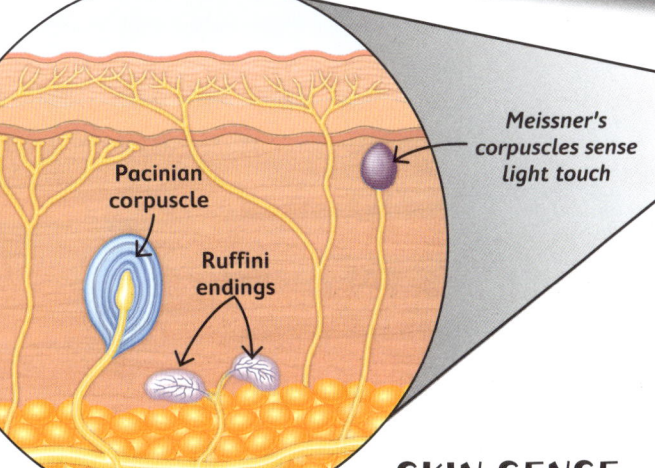

Pacinian corpuscle
Ruffini endings
Meissner's corpuscles sense light touch

SKIN SENSE

There are different receptors in your skin for pain, heat, cold, touch and pressure. Some, called Pacinian corpuscles, respond quickly and then stop. Others, called Ruffini endings, respond slowly then keep going.

◀ Your finger tips are so sensitive they can feel an object move if it only moves one thousandth of a millimetre.

To the rescue!

Your body often comes under attack by disease-causing bacteria, viruses and other germs. To fight these germs and keep you well, it has an array of biological weapons known as the immune system.

Body battles

Bacteria cause diseases such as whooping cough, tetanus, typhoid and TB.

Viruses cause diseases such as colds and flu, mumps, rabies and AIDS.

An **allergy** occurs when your body's defences overreact to a particular intruder.

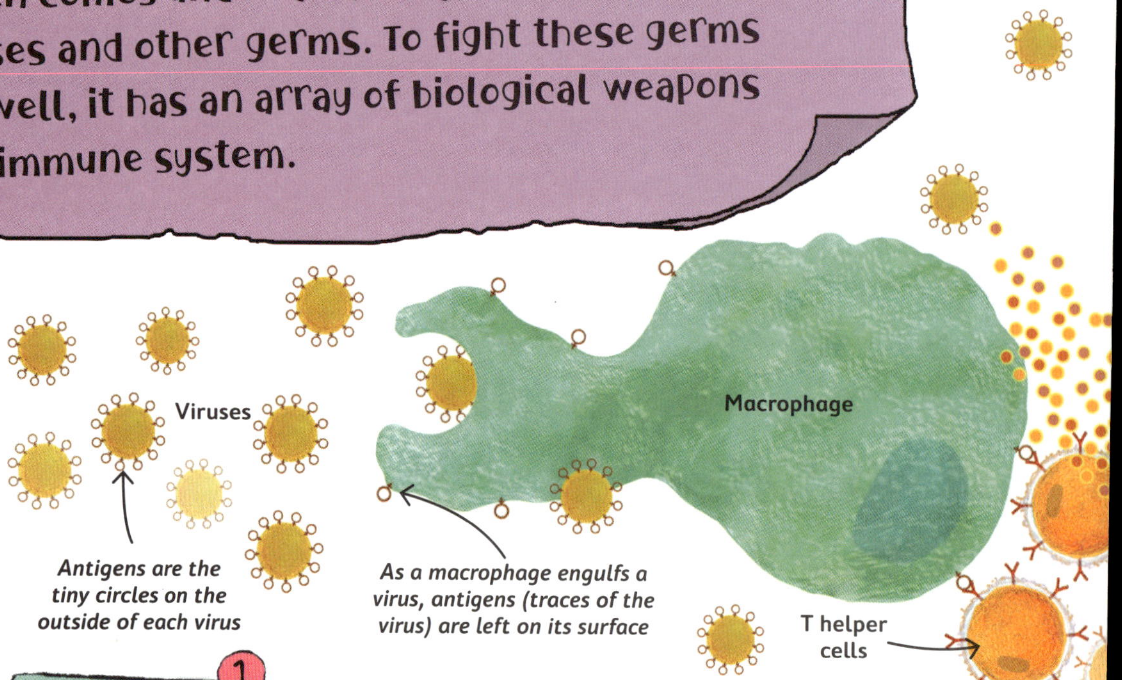

Viruses

Macrophage

Antigens are the tiny circles on the outside of each virus

As a macrophage engulfs a virus, antigens (traces of the virus) are left on its surface

T helper cells

1 Germs such as viruses that enter the body may be attacked by roving body cells called macrophages. Macrophages engulf a few viruses and kill them with toxic chemicals. Every germ has an identity tag on the outside called an antigen. When a macrophage engulfs a virus, it displays the virus's antigen on its surface.

2 White blood cells called T helpers have tags on their surface. If their tag matches the antigen on a macrophage, it locks on. Then it multiplies and sends out floods of chemicals that affect two more types of cells: B cells and T killers.

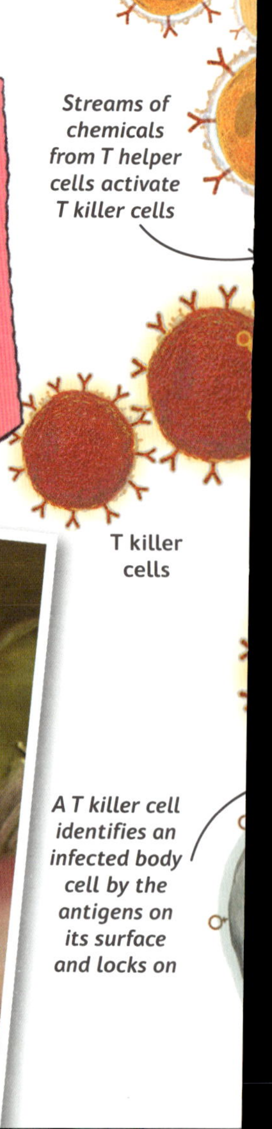

Streams of chemicals from T helper cells activate T killer cells

T killer cells

A T killer cell identifies an infected body cell by the antigens on its surface and locks on

AT THE GATES
Your body has outer defences to stop germs getting in. The first barrier is your skin. And if germs sneak in through your nose and lungs as you breathe they get bogged down in slimy mucus and blasted out with a cough or sneeze.

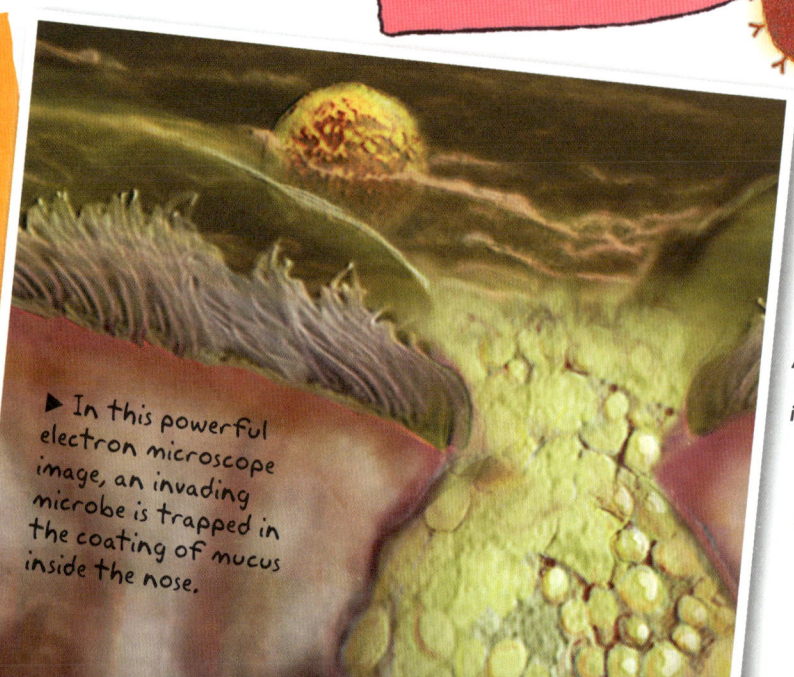

▶ *In this powerful electron microscope image, an invading microbe is trapped in the coating of mucus inside the nose.*

Make fake mucus

Mucus is made mostly of sugars and protein. Although different than the ones found in the real thing, you can use sugars and protein to make fake mucus.

SUPPLIES
green food colouring • cup of water • tablespoon
food supplement powder containing psyllium fibre
small plastic food box • microwave • spoon for stirring

HOW TO MAKE
1. Add a few drops of food colouring to the cup of water.
2. Place 1 tbsp of fibre powder in the food box.
3. Add the water to the fibre powder and stir slowly but thoroughly.
4. Place the box in a microwave and heat for three minutes. Remove, stir briefly and replace in the microwave for a further two minutes.
5. Let your mucus cool before squelching and stretching it – it should be fairly solid and very slimy. If it's still too liquid you can put it back in the microwave for a minute more – the longer it cooks, the more solid it will become.

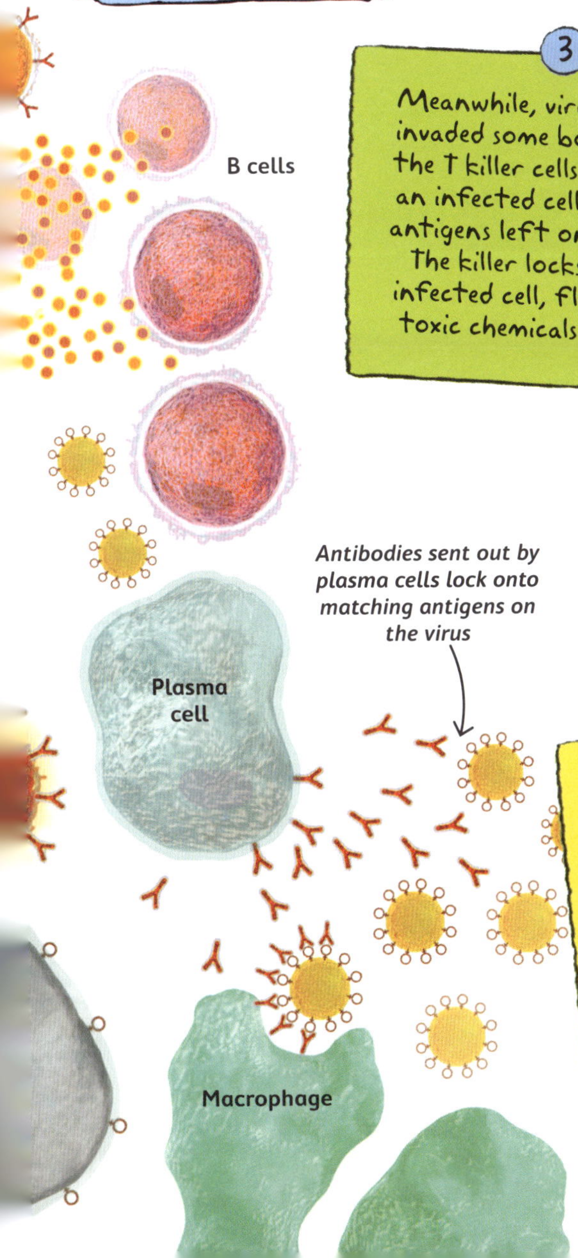

B cells

3 Meanwhile, viruses may have invaded some body cells. But the T killer cells can identify an infected cell by the virus antigens left on its surface. The killer locks on to the infected cell, floods it with toxic chemicals and kills it.

▼ Thanks to a worldwide campaign of vaccination, the terrible disease smallpox was finally eradicated in 1977.

There is a **different antibody** for every kind of germ.

Antibodies sent out by plasma cells lock onto matching antigens on the virus

Plasma cell

4 When a B cell encounters a virus it recognizes, it reacts to the chemicals sent out by the T helper. Some B cells become plasma cells, which make and send out antibodies. The antibodies lock onto the matching antigens of the virus. Viruses marked with antibodies are at high risk of being engulfed by macrophages, and may also be damaged by the antibodies themselves.

Macrophage

TARGET MODE
A vaccine infects you with a harmless form of a germ. This triggers your body to make antibodies against the germ. So when a real infection comes along in the future your body is ready to make antibodies against the germ super-quick.

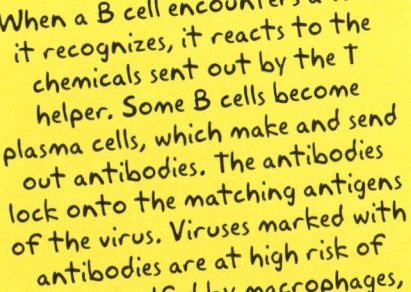

Train your brain

It's time to give your hippocampus a quick workout! This book contains all the information to answer these questions. Turn back through the pages if you need help remembering.

SCIENCE

1. kinetic energy (KE) is one kind of energy – can you name the other kind?
2. Which great scientist came up with three laws about motion in the 1600s?
3. What is the name of the mutual force of attraction that holds the Universe together?
4. When you squeeze water or air molecules into a smaller space, does the pressure rise or fall?
5. Planes fly by precisely balancing four things: thrust, drag, gravity, and what else?
6. What word beginning with 'l' is the fastest thing in the Universe?
7. At what temperature does water boil?
8. True or false: Things go rusty more quickly in saltwater than in freshwater.

SPACE

9. What name is given to the event that marked the beginning of the Universe – the Big Pop, or the Big Bang?
10. Which is hotter – a red star or a blue star?
11. Is the distance between galaxies measured in light years or dark years?
12. True or false: You are made of star dust.
13. What should you never look directly at – the Sun or the Moon?
14. Which planet is closest to the Sun?
15. True or false: Neptune take 16 years to travel around the Sun.
16. What is the name of the huge band of rocks that circle the Sun between Mars and Jupiter?

EARTH

17 True or false: The plates that make up Earth's crust move at a rate of up to 100 m each year.

18 Which volcano erupted in the year AD 79?

19 What word beginning with 'f' is the name of the place where an earthquake begins, deep underground?

20 Which ocean is bigger – the Southern Ocean or the Pacific Ocean?

21 What are the three states in which water can exist?

22 What kind of weather do cumulonimbus clouds signal?

23 Where does rubber come from?

BODY

24 What vitamin can your skin make from sunlight?

25 Do you breathe carbon dioxide in or out?

26 True or false: Pulmonary circulation carries blood through the liver.

27 What word beginning with 'v' is the name of the finger-like projections inside your small intestine?

28 Where does waste water go after it has been filtered by your kidneys?

29 How many hemispheres does your brain have?

30 Which part of your eye gives it its colour – the pupil or the iris?

ANSWERS

1. Potential energy (PE) 2. Sir Isaac Newton 3. Gravity 4. The pressure rises 5. Lift 6. Light 7. 100°C 8. True 9. The Big Bang 10. A blue star 11. Light years 12. True 13. The Sun 14. Mercury 15. False – it takes 165 years 16. The Asteroid Belt 17. False – they move at a rate of up to 10 cm each year 18. Mount Vesuvius 19. The focus 20. The Pacific Ocean 21. Solid, liquid and gas 22. Rain, possibly thunderstorms 23. From rubber trees 24. Vitamin D 25. You breathe carbon dioxide out 26. False – it carries blood through the lungs 27. Villi 28. To your bladder 29. Two 30. The iris

Index

Page numbers in **bold** refer to main subjects.

A
absolute zero 14
acceleration 15, **16**, **17**, 19
acids 29, **33**
aerofoils 23
air 92
    pressure 20, **21**, 96, 97
    resistance 19
anemometers 96
Apollo 51, 70
arteries 112, 113
asteroids 57, **66–67**
astronauts 70
atmosphere 74, 75, 90, 92, 102, 104
atoms **24–25**, **26**, 28, 33, 34, 37, 38
aurorae **37**

B
balance 122, 125, 131
barometers 96, 97
batteries 34, 35
Big Bang **46–47**, 75
biomes 86–89
black holes 55
bladder 116
blood 110, **112–113**
bones **120–123**, 131
brain 116, **124–125**, 132
breathing **110–111**
buoyancy **22**, 23

C
capillaries 113
caring for the Earth 102–103
cartilage 122
caves 91
chemical reactions **32–33**
circulation (blood) **112–113**
climate change 97, 102, **104–105**
clouds 79, 93
cochlea 131
combustion 32, 33
comets **68–69**
compass 37

compounds **26**, 27
continental drift 76
convection currents 77, 92
coral reefs 82
crust 76, 77
Curiosity rover 70–71

D
decibels 40
deserts 87
diaphragm 111
digestion **114–115**
diseases 134
drag 23
droughts 105
dust 44, 47, 48, 52–53, 54, 68

E
ears **130–131**
Earth 56, 57, 58, 59, 62, 63
earthquakes **80–81**
echolocation **40**
eclipse of the Sun 61
electricity 25, 27, 29, 31, **34–35**, 36, 93, 98, 100, 101
electromagnets **36**
electrons 24, 25, 34, 35
elements **26–29**
El Niño 104
energy **14–15**, 24, 37, 38, 74, 90, 93, **100–101**
evolution 84, 85
explosions 33
eyes **128–129**

F
farming 99
fireworks 32–33
floating **22**, 30
floods 79, 82, 91, 105
flying **23**
forces 16, 17, 19, 20, 22, **23**, 25, 36
fossil fuels 100, 102
freezing 30, 31
freshwater habitats 89

G
galaxies **50–51**, **54–55**
gas 44, 47, 48, 52–53, 60, 68
gases 30, 31, 32
gassy planets **64–65**
geothermal energy 101
geysers 20
global warming 104, 105

grasslands 86
gravity 14, 15, 17, **18–19**, 23, 25, 45, 58, 66, 75
Great Red Spot 64
greenhouse gases 104
gut **114–115**

H
hailstones 92, 95
hair 108, 109
Halley's Comet 69
healing 109, 123
heart **112–113**
heat energy **14**, 15
hurricanes and typhoons 95

I
ice 8, 9, 11, 23, 104, 105
immune system 112, **134–135**
International Space Station 70
iris 128

J, K
joints 120–123, 132
Jupiter 57, 58, 59, 64, 65, 66
kidneys 116, 117
kinetic energy (KE) **14**, 15

L
large intestine 114, 115
Laws of Motion **16–17**
lens 128
leptons 25
life on Earth 60, 63, 75, 82, 83, **84–85**, **86–89**
lift 23
light energy 37, **38–39**
lightning 35, 41, 93
light years 50
liquids **30**, 31, 32
liver 115
lungs **110–111**

M
magma 78
magnetic fields 36, 37
magnetism **36–37**
magnetosphere 37
mantle 76, 77, 78
Mars 56, 58, 59, 62, 63, 67, 70, 71
mass 18, **19**
matter 18, 24, 30–31
Mercury 56, 58, 59, 62, 63

138

metals 27, 28, 29, 31, 32, 33, 41, 98, 99
meteorites 67
meteoroids 67
meteorologists 96
meteors 67
Mid-Atlantic Ridge 76
Milky Way **54–55**
molecules 14, 20, **24**, 26, **30**, 31
momentum 15, 16, 18
Moon **45**, 56, 75
    eclipse of the Sun 61
    landing on the 70
moons of the planets 56, 57, 58, 59
motion **16–17**
mountains 88, 91
mucus 114, 134
mudflows 79
muscles 110, 112, **118–119**, 122, 132

N
nails 108
nebulae **52–53**
Neptune 57, 58, 59, 64, 65
nerve cells (neurons) 124, 126, 127
nervous system **126–127**
neutrons 24, 25
noble gases 27, 29
nose 132, 133

O
oceans 75, 76, 77, 81, **82–83**, 89, 102
Olympus Mons volcano 56, 62
orbits 18
oxygen 110, 111, 112, 113

P, Q
Periodic Table **26–29**
periscopes 39
photons **38**
pitch 40, 41
planes 22, 23, 41
planets 47, **56–59**
    gassy **64–65**
    rocky **62–63**
plasma **31**
plate tectonics **76–77**, 80
Pluto 59, 69, 70
polar regions 86, 94, 104
pollution 102

potato battery 101
potential energy (PE) **14**, 15
proprioceptors 132
protons 24, 25, 26, 34
pupil 128
quarks 25

R
radiation **38**, 74, 104
rain 87, 91, 92, 95
rainbows 38
rare earths 29
reflection **39**
reflexes 127
refraction 38, **39**
renewable energy **15**, 105
resources **98–99**, 102
respiration 110
retina 128, 129
ribcage 121
rings of Saturn 64
rock cakes 99
rockets 16–17, 71
rocks 76, 78, 99
rocky planets **62–63**
rubber 98
rust **32**

S
salt water 83
sandstorms 95
satellite data 96, 97
Saturn 58, 59, 64, 65
seasons 74
seismometers 80, 81
semi-circular canals 131
senses 124, **130–131**, **132–133**
shooting stars 67
sight **128–129**, 132
skeleton **120–123**
skin **108–109**, 133, 134
skull 120, 121
small intestine 114, 115
smell 125, 132, 133
snow 92, 94, 95
solar energy 15
solar flares 60
solar power 100
Solar System 55, **56–59**, 69, 75
    exploring the 70
solids 30, 31, 32
sonic boom 41
sound **40–41**, 130, 131, 132
sound waves **40**, 41
space **44–45**

spacecraft 62, **70–71**
spectrum 38
speed of light **38**
speed of sound **41**
Sputnik 1 70
stars 47, **48–49**, 50, 52, 53, 54
static electricity **34**, 35
stomach 114, 115
storms 94, 95, 105
sub-atomic particles **24**, 25
submersibles 83
Sun 48, 49, 56, 57, 59, **60–61**, 74, 75, 92, 100
supernova 49

T
taste 132, 133
telescopes 44, 62, 65, 70, 71
temperate regions 87
temperature **14**, 31, 95
terminal velocity 19
thrust 23
tides and waves 75, 81, 82
tongue 118, 133
tornadoes 94, 95
touch 132, 133
tropical forests 88
tsunamis 81
tundra 89

U, V
Universe **46–47**, 70
Uranus 58, 59, 64, 65
urine 116, 117
vaccination 135
veins 112, 113
Venus 56, 58, 59, 62, 63
volcanoes 56, 62, 63, **78–79**

W
water balance 116
water cycle **90–91**
waterfalls 91
water pressure **20**, 21
weather 79, 86, 92, **94–95**
    balloons 96
    systems 21
white blood cells 134
white light 38
windpipe (trachea) 110, 111
wind power 100
winds 92, 94

ACKNOWLEDGEMENTS

The publishers would like to thank the following artists who have contributed to this book:

Cover Jack Viant (The Bright Agency)

Insides Julian Baker (J B Illustrations), Paul Boston (Meiklejohn Illustration), Peter Bull, Sara Lynn Cramb (Astound), Tom Heard (The Bright Agency), Sarah Horne (Advocate Art), Stuart Jackson-Carter, Rob McClurkan (The Bright Agency), Anne Passchier (The Bright Agency), Dan Taylor (The Bright Agency), Richard Watson (The Bright Agency), Tom Woolley (Astound US Inc)

All other artwork from the Miles Kelly Artwork Bank

The publishers would like to thank the following sources for the use of their photographs:
t = top, b = bottom, l = left, r = right, c = centre, m = main t = top, b = bottom,
bg = background, rt = repeated throughout

Alamy 33(bl) E. R. Degginger; 36(m) Bernd Mellmann; 81(t) Newscom; 96–97(m) RGB Ventures/SuperStock; 103(tr) Reuters; 110(bl) dpa picture alliance archive; 116–117(m) Tetra Images

ESA 97(cr) ESA—P. Carril

Getty 102–103(c) Roijoy/iStock

Glow 110–111(m) Pixologicstudio/Science Photo Library; 110(c) Sciepro/Science Photo Library; 115(bc) Sciepro/Science Photo Library; 126–127(m) Sciepro/Science Photo Library; 129(c) Steve Gschimeissner/Science Photo Library; 130–131(m) Science Picture Co/Superstock

NASA 18–19(m) NASA/JPL; 31(cr) ESA/NASA/SOHO; NASA 51 NASA, H. Fort (JHU), G. Illingworth (USCS/LO), M. Clampin (STScI), G. Hartig (STScI), the ACS Science Team, and ESA; 52–53 NASA, ESA, and M. Livio and the Hubble 60th Anniversary Team (STScI); 52 NASA, ESA and The Hubble Heritage Team (STScI/AURA); 53 NASA, ESA, J. Hester, A. Loll (ASU), (tc) Andrew Fruchter; 56(t) NASA/MOLA Science Team/ O. de Goursac, Adrian Lark, (c) NASA, JHU APL, CIW, (b) NASA/JPL; 57 NASA Jet Propulsion Laboratory (NASA-JPL); 58; 59(t) NASA/JPL, (c), (b) Thierry Lombry/NASA; 70–71 NASA/JPL-Caltech; 71(br) NASA, JPL-Caltech, Kate Su (Steward Obs, U. Arizona) et al.; 95(bl) UW-Madison/SSEC, William Straka III

Rex Features 19(br) Red Bull Content Pool/REX/Shutterstock; 61 KeystoneUSA-ZUMA

Science Photo Library 16–17(m) David Ducros, ESA; 21(b) University of Dundee; 24–25(m) Mik-kel Juul Jensen; 29(tl) Alexandre Dotta; 32(br) Andrew Lambert Photography; 44–45 Babak Tafreshi, Twan; 46–47 Jose Antonio Peñas; 48(b) Jose Antonio Peñas; 48–49(bg) Miguel Claro; 54–55 Mark Garlick; 56–59 Detlev Van Ravenswaay; 60–61 Henning Dalhoff; 67 Walter Pachol-ka, Astropics; 70 NASA; 71 NASA; 76(cl) NOAA; 78–79(c) Douglas Peebles; 80(c) Sputnik; 83(b) Sputnik; 84–85(c) Jose Antonio Penas; 112–113(m) Pixologicstudio; 114–115(m) Pixologicstu-dio; 119(c) Steve Gschmeissner; 124–125(m) Springer Medizin; 128–129(m) Jacopin/BSIP; 131(tl) Steve Gschmeissner; 133(c) Clouds Hill Imaging Ltd; 134(bc) Anatomical Travelogue; 135(cr) CDC

Shutterstock 14–15(m) Santiparp Wattanaporn; 19(bl) Ana del Castillo; 22(bl) XAOC; 24(bl) Orange Deer; 26(tl) Triff/Nasa, (br) EpicStockMedia; 27(bl) Omer Cicek, (c) T. Kimmeskamp, (bc) Zastolskiy Victor; 29(tr) Eric Boucher; 30(m) Sergey Nivens; 31(tl) e_rik, (cr) Nikolay Petkov; 35(t) kornilov0017; 37(cr) John A Davis; 38–39(m) XYZ; 41(t) Anatoliy Lukich; 44(br/rt) tanatat; 45 Rafael Pacheco; 55 John A Davis; 56(postcard rt) Irena Misevic; 67(tr) Action Sports Photography; 86–89(bg), 32(bg) iSiripong; 74(bl) Redsapphire; 74–75(c) Aphelleon/NASA; 75(tl) Eric Boucher; 76–77(c) Mopic; 79(br) Puripat Lertpunyaroj; 80(cr) Rainer Lesniewski; 82(bl) Vlad761; 82–83(c) EpicStockMedia; 86(tl) Graeme Shannon, (cr) DonLand; 87(tr) Jerry Zitterman, (tl) worldswildlifewonders, (tc) EcoPrint, (bl) Alexander Wong, (br) Kertu; 88(t) Karen Kane, (b) David Evison, (br) Dr Morley Read; 89(tl) Tom Middleton, (tr) Meister Photos, (b) Damsea; 91(br) David A Knight; 92(c) Vadim Sadovski, (b) Kichigin; 93(t) Vasin Lee; 94(c) Ipedan; 95(t) BCFC, (bc) Minerva Studio; 96(b) Svobodin Anton; 98–99(c) Andrey N Bannov; 99(b) Sergey Malov, (br) smereka; 100(c) artjazz; 101(c) Pavel Svoboda Photography; 104(m) FloridaStock; 105(t) Jag_cz; 108–109(m) Roman Chazov; 122(tl) I T A L O; 122–123(t) Suzan Oschmann; 123(r) Praisaeng

The Seabin Project 103(tr) The Team at Seabin Project

Every effort has been made to acknowledge the source and copyright holder of each picture.
Miles Kelly Publishing apologizes for any unintentional errors or omissions.